GETTING A JOB AFTE

How To Books on Jobs and Careers

Applying for a Job
Career Networking
Career Planning for Women
Finding a Job in Canada
Finding a Job in Computers
Finding a Job with a Future
Finding Work Overseas
Freelance DJ-ing
Freelance Teaching & Tutoring
Getting a Job After University
Getting Your First Job
How to Be a Freelance Journalist
How to Be a Freelance Sales Agent
How to Be a Freelance Secretary
How to Become an Au Pair
How to Do Voluntary Work Abroad
How to Find Temporary Work Abroad
How to Get a Job Abroad
How to Get a Job in America
How to Get a Job in Australia
How to Get a Job in Europe
How to Get a Job in France
How to Get a Job in Germany
How to Get a Job in Hotels & Catering
How to Get a Job in Travel & Tourism
How to Get Into Films & TV
How to Get Into Radio
How to Get That Job
How to Know Your Rights at Work
How to Manage Your Career
How to Market Yourself
How to Return to Work
How to Start a New Career
How to Work from Home
How to Work in an Office
How to Work in Retail
How to Work with Dogs
How to Write a CV That Works
Living & Working in China
Passing That Interview
Surviving Redundancy
Working as a Holiday Rep
Working in Japan
Working in Photography
Working on Contract Worldwide
Working on Cruise Ships
Working with Children
Working with Horses

Other titles in preparation

The How To Series now contains more than 200 titles in the following categories:

Business Basics
Family Reference
Jobs & Careers
Living & Working Abroad
Student Handbooks
Successful Writing

Please send for a free copy of the latest catalogue for full details (see back cover for address).

JOBS & CAREERS

GETTING A JOB AFTER UNIVERSITY

How to discover the right opportunities to meet your interests and needs

Sally Longson

Cartoons by Mike Flanagan

British Library Cataloguing in Publication Data
A catalogue record for this book is available from the British Library.

© Copyright 1997 by Sally Longson.

First published in 1997 by How To Books Ltd, 3 Newtec Place,
Magdalen Road, Oxford OX4 1RE, United Kingdom.
Tel: (01865) 793806. Fax: (01865) 248780.

All rights reserved. No part of this work may be reproduced or stored in an information retrieval system (other than for purposes of review) without the express permission of the Publisher in writing.

Note: The material contained in this book is set out in good faith for general guidance and no liability can be accepted for loss or expense incurred as a result of relying in particular circumstances on statements made in the book. The laws and regulations are complex and liable to change, and readers should check the current position with the relevant authorities before making personal arrangements.

Produced for How To Books by Deer Park Productions.
Typeset by PDQ Typesetting, Stoke-on-Trent, Staffs.
Printed and bound by Cromwell Press, Broughton Gifford, Melksham, Wiltshire.

Contents

List of illustrations		8
Preface		9
1	**Making plans**	11
	The future: scary, exciting or both?	11
	Setting time aside	12
	Getting information as you go	15
	Coping with pressure	17
	Keeping an open mind	17
	Making decisions	18
	Making an action plan	19
	Getting help from the careers service	19
	Remember!	22
	Case studies	22
	Discussion points	23
2	**Taking stock**	24
	Identifying your skills	24
	Relating your skills and interests to jobs	29
	Identifying your potential	31
	Adding your personal touch	34
	Increasing your knowledge base	34
	Case studies	34
	Discussion points	35
3	**Getting in touch with reality**	36
	Getting in touch with work	36
	Finding where you fit in	40
	Understanding your options in work	41
	You've got more choice	42
	Don't forget small firms!	44
	Summary	45
	Case studies	45
	Discussion points	46

4	**Establishing your needs and values**	47
	Defining happiness and success	47
	How far do you want to go?	49
	Thinking about size and location	51
	Learning more	52
	Take five: give me a break!	54
	A chance to work abroad	55
	Earning money	55
	Thinking about your non-financial values	57
	Being independent	57
	Case studies	59
	Discussion points	60
5	**Showing the right attitude and image**	61
	Acquiring the right attitude	61
	How healthy is your attitude?	62
	Helping yourself	63
	Thinking about your image	65
	Summary	67
	Case studies	67
	Discussion points	67
6	**Looking for work**	69
	Some first thoughts	69
	Networking	69
	Networking via information	73
	Writing to employers	76
	Signing up with recruitment agencies	79
	Attending organised events	81
	Working for yourself	82
	Finding work abroad	83
	More tips on getting a job	84
	Case studies	85
	Discussion points	86
7	**Marketing yourself**	87
	Getting ready	87
	Making contact	88
	Writing your covering letter and CV	89
	Completing the application form	93
	Coping with the interview	97
	Coping with the next round	102
	Remember	104
	Case studies	104
	Discussion points	105

8	**Dealing with common barriers and obstacles**	106
	Coping with rejection	106
	Lacking work experience	106
	Dealing with 'no vacancy' and no response	109
	Thinking about age	110
	Overcoming prejudice	111
	Being over-qualified	112
	Disabilities	112
	Handling pressure	112
	Finding it hard to get a placement	113
	Summary	113
	Case studies	114
	Discussion points	114
9	**Coping with unemployment or underemployment**	115
	Expecting it	115
	Being single-minded	116
	Keeping busy	116
	Getting there... by hook or by crook	117
	Keeping the job market in mind	121
	Summary	122
	Case studies	122
	Discussion points	122
10	**The route to being employed**	123
	Starting work	123
	Preparing for your future	124
	Learning – will it never end?	126
	Redundancy – will it happen to me?	127
	Summary	129
	Case studies	129
	Discussion points	130
Glossary		131
Useful addresses		134
Further reading		136
Index		139

List of Illustrations

1	Thinking and planning ahead	14
2	Which way now?	16
3	Making an action plan	20
4	Skills acquired inter-railing	28
5	Academic activities develop transferable skills	28
6	IT provides many career opportunities	38
7	Original career choice	42
8	The way forward looks different now	43
9	Specialising	50
10	Examples of perks	56
11	Action plan for writing on spec	64
12	Portraying the right image	66
13	Networking helps	70
14	Writing on spec	78
15	Writing a covering letter	90
16	Writing a CV	94
17	'Keep me in mind' letter	108
18	Virtuous and vicious circles	116
19	Avenues to information	120
20	Training means increased job prospects	128

Preface

When I graduated in the mid-1980s, life was very different for graduates. I remember well our graduation day at Bangor (well, most of it). Actually, I hadn't visited the careers service there while I was a student, but then I had never made use of any of the careers services available to me while I was in full-time education. I often wonder how different my life would have been if I had, although I have enjoyed my career – it's been extremely satisfying, international and exhilarating throughout. I hope you make better use of the services available to you – they are a mine of information, help and support.

In the 1990s, however, things are different. For a start, there are far more students going through higher education. Job security is a thing of the past. There is also a wide variety of options available after graduation. I hope this book will help you find the right path, whether you've left university or you're still there.

Two points to bear in mind: this book refers most often to university but relates to graduates from colleges and institutes also; it refers to 'university' solely for ease of reference. Likewise, it refers frequently to 'he, his' rather than 'she, her', also for ease of reference and to save the reader from laboriously ploughing through lots of he/she, he or she *etc*.

I'd like to thank: Dr Roger Hughes and the staff at Queen Mary and Westfield College Careers Service for their help and letting me use their library; Roger Ferneyhough for asking me to write the book; the employers I've worked with over the years who've commented often on what they look for in a recruit, from the skills they have to the way students market themselves; and the students, who've been searching for the right job at the right time. I must also thank David Greenwood, whose advice has aways been so willingly and thoughtfully given, and in particular my parents, who through their example showed me that self-employment is possible. Most of all, I'd like to thank my partner, Paul, for his wonderful and continuous encouragement, support and enthusiasm from the day I started to write.

Sally Longson

IS THIS YOU?

Graduate

Unemployed   Underemployed

Ambitious

Anxious   Positive

Uncertain

In debt   Career-minded

Open-minded

Employable   Hopeful

Despairing

Job applicant   Student

Job seeker

Post-graduate   Mature student

Interviewee

Taking a year out   Changing career

Wanting to work abroad

Portfolio person   Wanting to be self-employed

Freelancer

Over-qualified   Well-qualified

Professional

1
Making Plans

THE FUTURE: SCARY, EXCITING OR BOTH?

This book is about getting a job after university. As a participant in higher education, you want all your hard work to lead to something, presumably a job if you are reading this book. News headlines highlight the general lack of job security in the 1990s, increased pressure and stress at work, and concern about the quality of education standards today. Your worries about the graduate employment market have increased since you've seen several of last year's graduates still hanging around campus saying they can't get work. Most people know a graduate somewhere who is still looking for a job.

Mixed messages
There have been mixed messages about the demand for graduates.

- 'Britain needs more graduates in order to compete with other countries.'
- 'Is Britain producing too many graduates?'
- 'There are opportunities out there – it's a matter of looking for them.'
- 'There aren't any jobs out there for people without experience.'
- 'It may take you time to get the sort of position you want.'

The good news
- Employers want people with the right skills, attitude and personal qualities.
- Many vacancies are filled not through advertising but by other methods.
- Graduate vacancies are on the increase.

But what of job security?
There are no more jobs for life. To be employed, you need to:

- know what you want to achieve and plan accordingly
- understand the job market

- have the ability to find opportunities
- know how to market yourself
- know when the time is right to move on.

In the last chapter of this book, there'll be advice on how to make sure you can be employed for life. But right now, what of the immediate future?

Is this what you think?

I know what I want to do after university and I think my course has been a good preparation for work.	Yes/No
I can't face thinking about my career while I've got so much to do here. I'll decide later. I'll have more time then.	Yes/No
I want time out to recover after all this – then I'll look for a job.	Yes/No
I want to travel before starting my career. I'll work to pay off my overdraft first though.	Yes/No
I'll do accountancy/teaching/law as a career – they're fairly straightforward – it'll save time thinking about it. Now I can stop worrying and it'll get everyone off my back.	Yes/No
I don't even know where to start. When I think about leaving university, I feel as though I've hit a brick wall. I've not got a clue about what I want to do.	Yes/No
I've graduated! I wanted to concentrate on my studies and get a good degree, then decide. Where can I get help?	Yes/No

Other (state): _____

SETTING TIME ASIDE

University days sneak by quickly. Before you know it, you've moved from Freshers' Week to finals, and all the talk in the student bar is about interviews, exhibitions and hair cuts. And among all the pressures of study, money, fitting in extra-curricular activities and working part time, there's **career planning** to think about. After all, it takes time to:

- attend career interviews
- do research
- write up CVs

- write letters of application
- complete application forms
- attend interviews
- sort out funding (if you are doing a post-graduate degree)

especially if you are really committed to getting a job. It will also cost you money (*eg* telephone, postage, photocopying, clothes, travelling to interviews).

Finding time for career planning

Look at your week now
Take a typical week and record how you spend time hour by hour, whether it's the holidays, you've left university or you're in the middle of the term.

Where are you wasting time?
Can you find any hours where you've wasted time through, for example:

chatting	worrying
watching TV	forgetting things
moaning and groaning	thinking about it instead of doing it
being hungover	procrastinating through fear of failing or not being good enough

Allocating time to career planning

Make up a new **timetable**. Put in necessities, *eg* lectures, labs, tutorials and allocate time for private study, career planning, working part time and other activities which will enhance your CV, and stick to it. The more effectively you manage time, the more you can fit in.

Make use of vacation time

Holidays can provide very useful opportunities to:

- research career options

- make contact with your local Training and Enterprise Council (TEC) to see what services they offer

- get paid/unpaid experience, *eg* temping, voluntary work, travel

- do some networking, *eg* with past school friends, friends of the family

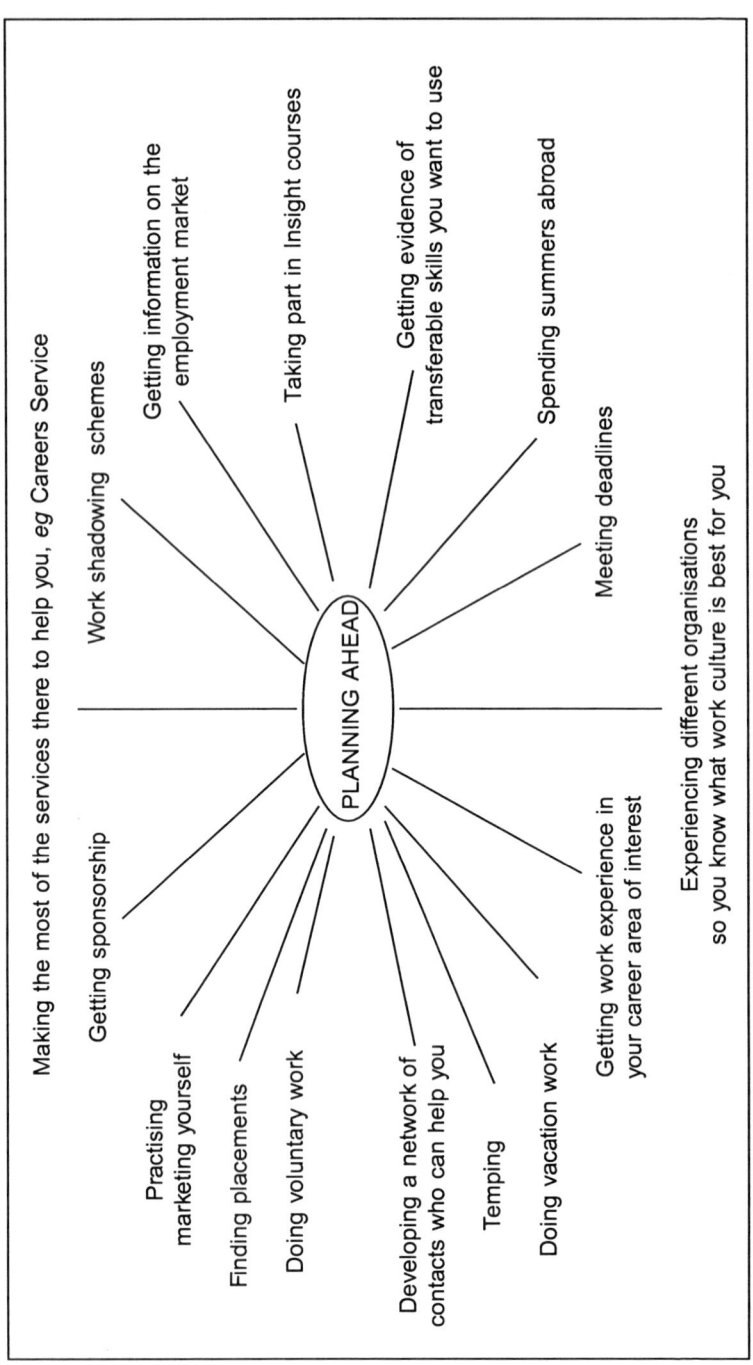

Fig. 1. Thinking and planning ahead.

- pay off your overdraft.

Not at university and unemployed?
Make out a similar timetable. It will help you establish a routine. Make career planning your focal point, but include any activities which an employer will look favourably upon, such as voluntary work, training available through your local TEC, any job search programmes it offers and keeping fit.

Make use of spare time
Even if you are unemployed, employers like to see that you've spent your spare time constructively. It shows that you have energy, drive and motivation, because you've actually chosen to do something active, rather than just stay in all day and watch television. It also shows that when the going gets tough, you can handle it – another characteristic employers like in an increasingly competitive and pressurised work environment.

GETTING INFORMATION AS YOU GO

Start a career management file
Use this file continually to build up a **portfolio** of information about you, the job market and ways to find a job, whether or not you have graduated. Put everything you write connected with your career into this file and add to it constantly. Information is power.

By building up such a file continually, you can:

- keep records of your activities and achievements in academic life, extra-curricular activities or employment – it will be much easier to remember them

- save time in searching for bits of paper strewn over your flat/room

- keep cuttings of articles about the employment market, *eg* trends, vacancies, cuttings of companies that you might work for, new ways to find work.

Killing two birds with one stone
Making career decisions takes time. Planning ahead buys you time because you know what you need to do (see Figure 1).

Your studies, career planning activities, work experience (paid/unpaid/voluntary), extra-curricular activities and new skills learnt after

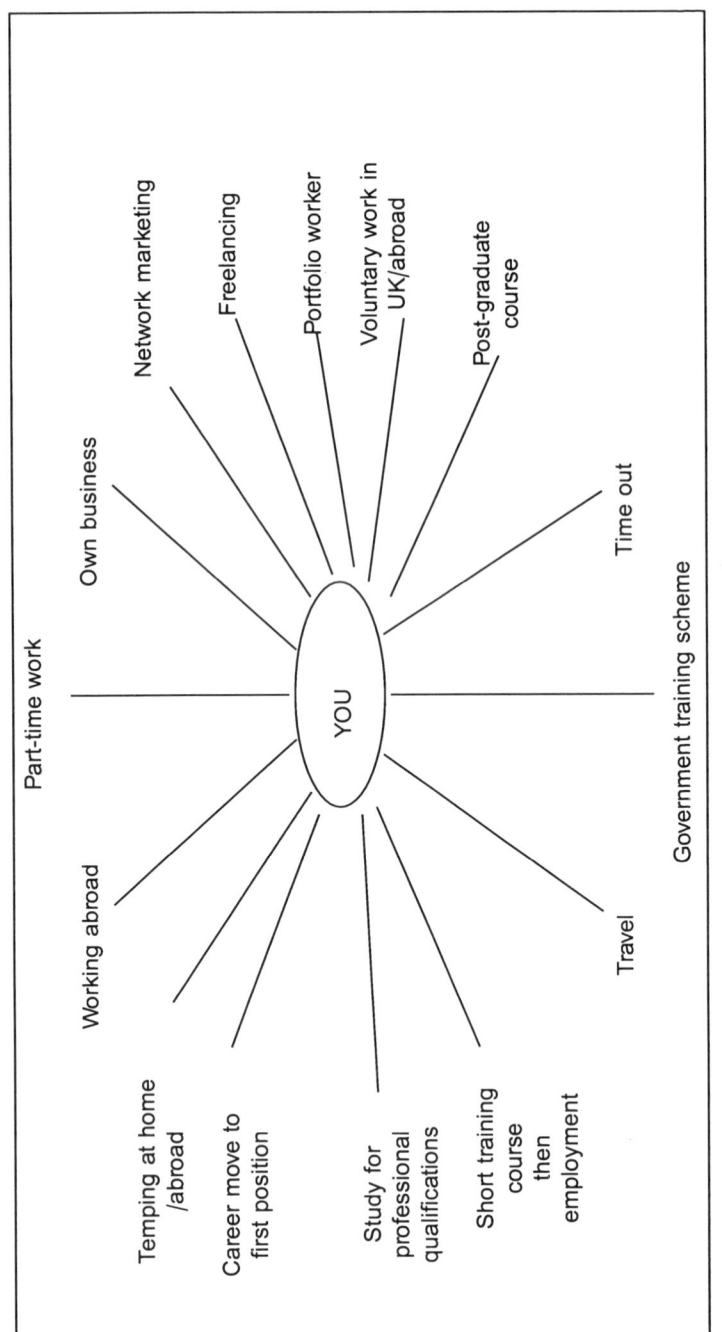

Fig. 2. Which way now?

Making Plans

leaving university can all contribute to your future career if you understand how they relate to employment and if you sell them correctly.

COPING WITH PRESSURE

Saying goodbye
When you start university, you expect to experience culture shock as you adjust to a new lifestyle. When you leave, you may experience **exit shock** as you say goodbye to friends, university staff, the surroundings, university life and perhaps full-time education. Life won't be the same again: 'It's over!'

Meeting expectations
You've invested several years of your life in this course and everyone wants to know what you're going to do afterwards. People you know are waiting with interest to see what you're going to do after all this study. Plus you have to deal with your debts.

Manage your stress level
1. Talk to people who will listen and be constructive.
2. Keep fit – exercise relieves stress and makes you sharper mentally.
3. Get plenty of sleep.
4. Don't alleviate stress by excess drinking.
5. Set yourself achievable goals.
6. Plan your study time carefully.
7. Don't leave things to the last minute.
8. Get help with areas of study that are difficult for you early on.
9. Expect change – it will be less of a surprise when it occurs!

KEEPING AN OPEN MIND

This is a book about job hunting. It assumes you want to get a job straight after your degree, rather than continue on to post-graduate study. As you research your options, however, you may find that your proposed career path is best served by studying for a post-graduate qualification, in which case you'll need to look at post-graduate courses, or indeed one of the choices indicated in Figure 2.

Working has pros and cons
Pros
- Regular salary coming in – can start paying off overdraft.

- Can do further study and training part-time.
- Can develop skills in work.
- Excitement of moving on to a new lifestyle, meeting new people.

Cons
- Could take time to find the job you want.
- May need to get some experience or a post-graduate degree to get into the field you want.
- May feel you are underemployed.
- Leaving the known environment of education could be a shock.
- Working costs money!

Questions and answers
I don't know what I'm going to do after my course and I haven't got the slightest idea how to decide. I don't even know what I could do with my degree. Please help! What should I do?
It's a daunting task to make career plans because there are so many choices available. Start with YOU – your likes, interests, strengths and values. A careers counsellor can guide you through the decision-making process, but don't expect to make a decision about your career within the space of one interview. It takes time to make an informed career choice.

I've done a vocational course – architecture – but I've changed my mind about being an architect. Will I be able to change career or is it too late?
It's not too late. You will need to convince prospective employers of your reasons for changing your career plans and show them that you've researched your new career path thoroughly, *eg* through work experience, visits, attending talks, meeting trainees *etc*.

I know what I want to do but I need a couple of years' experience first, 'doing anything with a wide variety of people'. Any suggestions?
Talk to recruitment personnel in your chosen field to find out what specific skills and qualities they want in a recruit and then find methods for developing these. Talk to people in that line of work. What did they do? What concrete plans would they suggest?

MAKING DECISIONS

Career choice will affect your **lifestyle**, *eg* location, travel opportunities, hours you put in, what you can afford to do, clothes you wear, satisfaction you get, opportunities available. You need to know how important these sorts of values and needs are to *you*, although once in work, original values such as normal working hours can quickly become irrelevant in the excitement and pressure of it all.

How?
People make decisions in different ways:

- careful thought and research
- instinct and intuition – they know instinctively what they want to do
- tossing a coin and trusting to luck
- force of circumstance, *eg* they were made redundant
- following the lead or example of others, *eg* their friends are doing it
- fear – they delay so much they are forced to make a rapid decision and can fall back on the 'Well, I didn't research this properly, anyway' excuse.

Do any of these apply to you?

'Do I have to think about it?'
Many people put off making career decisions because of the following fears:

Common fears	*Is this you?*
Making the wrong decision	Yes/No
Failure	Yes/No
What will others think?	Yes/No
The application process	Yes/No
A lack of confidence	Yes/No
Not knowing where to start!	Yes/No

MAKING AN ACTION PLAN

The action plan in Figure 3 outlines the career decision-making process. It can be used wherever you are at in your career thoughts.

GETTING HELP FROM THE CAREERS SERVICE

Services vary throughout the UK, but include university/college careers services, those originally run by local education authorities which have now been privatised and private companies not connected with government at all.

Trained, professional careers counsellors will discuss your future with you impartially and confidentially. They will help you identify

You may have already used a similar action plan before, *eg* when deciding what course to do at university and where to do it. You will need to work your way through action plans like this throughout your entire life – even in retirement – to keep in tune with changing circumstances and aspirations.

Self-knowledge
(Chapters 2, 4, 5)

Checklist:
1. Your strengths, interests, likes, ambitions, career aspirations, values, needs and skills that you would like to use.
2. Your weaknesses and dislikes.
3. What you want out of life and what success and happiness mean to you.
4. How your wishes relate to others, *eg* family, partner, friends.

Opportunity awareness
(Chapters 3, 6)

Relate your self-knowledge to opportunities:
1. In employment and training
2. In post-graduate education
3. Locally, nationally and internationally
4. Employment trends

Decision-making
(Chapters 1-10)

Develop your decision-making skills:
1. Communication
2. Research
3. Analysing information
4. Time management
5. Understanding the process involved
6. Ways to find work

Transition skills
(Chapters 7, 8, 9, 10)

Make the move:
1. Selection methods
2. Marketing yourself
3. Applying effectively
4. Starting
5. Making an impact
6. Knowing when to move on

Fig. 3. Making an effective plan.

your skills and interests and match them up with possible career areas. Counsellors and advisers work closely with employers and higher education providers, strengthening the link between industry and education and seeking to help employers to fill vacancies and students to locate them.

University careers services

These services are ideally placed to help you. Use them **early on** in your university career – most will still help after you leave for a period of time. They vary in their services, but most will:

- have information about employment trends, graduate trends, different employers, post-graduate courses and prospectuses, application forms, work experience or shadowing programmes, working abroad, the background to different careers, details of professional bodies
- run courses or group sessions on a variety of subjects *eg* 'Interview technique' or more specifically, 'A career in...'
- keep destination statistics of past graduates to show you what they have done and put you in touch with those in your career area of interest
- provide computer-aided guidance systems such as Prospects, Adult Directions, Gradscope
- offer you practice in taking psychometric tests
- run a vacancy service, whereby employers notify the service of vacancies and even arrange to visit campus: (a) to give students more information about themselves through a presentation and (b) to interview prospective recruits.

If you start career planning while you are at university, it will be easier as you should have convenient access to a careers service. Some services may charge for services such as counselling after you have left.

Get to know your university careers service
Visit your careers service and find your way around so that you become familiar with the staff and resources there and the opening times, and know of forthcoming events and talks that may help you.

Local careers services
Recently privatised, these tend to focus on young people leaving school

or college but again this varies throughout Britain. However, services can provide information on:

- the local labour market which should be up to date
- local vacancies
- employers you could talk to
- opportunities for self-employment.

Check with your local careers service or Training and Enterprise Council (TEC) (see *Yellow Pages*) to see what help they can offer you. Vacations could be a good time to make contact and do some career planning, especially if you want to work in your home town.

Privatised careers services
You pay for these. They usually offer the chance to discuss your strengths, weaknesses, interests and needs with a consultant and match them to career opportunities. Some offer interviews with a psychologist plus the chance to do computer-aided tests.

REMEMBER!

- A variety of activities can contribute to your career planning if you analyse them for transferable skills.
- They also provide evidence of the skills and qualities you can offer, *eg* motivation.
- Different firms have different deadlines for application. You don't want to miss any crucial dates.
- Use any opportunity to learn about careers, *eg* courses run by organisations to give you an insight into careers with them.

CASE STUDIES

Here are three different students at university, all with different fears and plans for the future. The book will follow their progress chapter by chapter.

Sarah studies Business Studies and Drama
Sarah was very nervous about going to university, but feels the experience has developed her confidence. She chose drama and business studies because she enjoyed them at school but she has no

career plans, although she graduates in six months. Her work experience consists of baby-sitting and a summer job doing market research questionnaires for a local company, which she enjoyed. 'I'm concentrating on my studies,' Sarah tells friends and family, 'I'll look for work after I graduate.' Deep down, she becomes increasingly anxious about leaving full-time education with no firm path forward.

Matthew is a history graduate

Matthew's passion is history. He spent the summer holidays working at a local castle as a guide and sales assistant. As President of the History Society in his second year, he led an active committee of eight, which organised visiting speakers, outings and a club Christmas party. Matthew thought he wanted to be an accountant after spending three summers working for accountancy firms in his home town, so he visited the careers office in his second year to find out about the application process.

Mary is a mature student

Mary started her degree course after her children had all begun school. She enjoyed her sociology course and wanted to work with children after her degree was over. That meant staying in the area, because the children were happy and her husband had a good position in a large local company. Mary was worried because she couldn't imagine an employer taking her on at the age of 42. She went to see the careers service in her second week at university and talked to a careers adviser about her worries. Together, they worked out a strategy.

DISCUSSION POINTS

1. What benefits can you get from talking to other students about their career plans?

2. How important is self-awareness in career planning?

3. How different is the process of choosing your university course from that of choosing your career path now?

2
Taking Stock

Questions and answers

What skills can I develop at university that would be useful to an employer?
The skills employers look for vary in emphasis from one organisation to another, but they all want qualities and skills in addition to a qualification. Evidence of these transferable skills and qualities can be provided from a range of activities at university, *eg* studies, part-time employment and extra-curricular activities.

I find it really difficult to sell myself – how can I overcome this fear?
Many people dislike identifying their assets and achievements because they are shy or lack confidence – but **do it you must** so that you know what you have to offer to a prospective employer. If you look for evidence of these skills, the process becomes easier, *eg* 'I promoted the play and we got a full house every night'. Putting values and scales to things makes them easier to shout about!

When am I supposed to develop all these skills?
Activities you do as part of your course help you to develop the transferable skills and intellectual abilities employers want. This also applies to part-time work you do to fund yourself, work experience which gives you a broader insight into the workplace and extra-curricular activities which prove your motivation and energy.

IDENTIFYING YOUR SKILLS

Look at advertisements or through careers literature. You will frequently see demands for **transferable skills**, *ie* skills that will travel with you and transfer from one activity to another. These may include the following:

Managing yourself
Can you:
- meet deadlines?
- identify priorities?
- work without supervision?
- take responsibility for your own career development and planning?
- understand employment patterns and how they relate to you?
- recognise when it is time to move on?
- identify yourself – your strengths, interests, values and needs?

Managing projects
Can you:
- plan?
- work with others to get things done?
- meet deadlines?
- complete projects as required?

Managing change?
Can you:
- implement change?
- respond to change?
- contribute to and shape change?
- convince others of the need to change?
- suggest change?

Leadership
Can you:
- guide and motivate others?
- persuade them over to your viewpoint?
- be energetic and enthusiastic in encouraging the team to excel?

Analysing skills
Can you:
- identify issues?
- research topics?
- handle lots of complex information?
- identify relevant details?
- interpret the facts?
- draw logical conclusions?
- support views with evidence?
- question things rather than accept them at face value?

Communication skills
Can you:
- speak clearly and articulately?
- write with good grammar and spelling?
- give presentations to a variety of audiences?
- listen attentively?
- think on your feet?
- be persuasive and sensitive to others?

Team member
- When have you worked as part of a team?
- What was your contribution?
- What role do you prefer to play?
- What roles in a team would be of interest?
- Can you establish a working relationship with others quickly?

Planning and organising
- Can you identify something you planned?
- Have you organised anything?
- How did it go?
- What would you do differently next time?

Problem-solving
- Can you identify a problem you solved?
- How did you approach it?
- What barriers did you have to overcome?
- What was the outcome?

Receptiveness to training and learning
- Are you motivated to learn more?
- Do you grasp things quickly?
- Can you learn without direction?

Initiative and drive
- Can you suggest new ideas?
- Do you like to exceed your targets?
- What have you done to show an employer you don't just sit at home and watch television?
- Are you competitive?
- Are you determined to overcome problems?

Business awareness
- Can you show an understanding of how business operates?
- Do you set yourself targets?
- Do you know how external forces can influence a company?
- Can you think strategically?
- Can you recognise internal politics and handle them?

You've been taught to think differently
Employers seeking graduates in 'any discipline' want recruits for their intellectual competence and ability to learn, rather than for their knowledge of a subject. Do you look at things differently now and question them, *eg* 'What if we did it this way?' 'What if this happened?' You can spot different ways to do things. You can interact with a wide variety of people at all levels. You can cope with anything thrown at you.

Analysing your skills
List your achievements and activities:

- topics you've covered
- methods of learning you've used, *eg* seminars, tutorials, lectures, presentations, visits, projects, essays, debates, assignments *etc* and star those that are relevant to the workplace (topics and methods)
- work experience (paid, unpaid, voluntary, part of university course, part/full-time)
- positions of responsibility.

Keep this list in your career management file, along with all other information you acquire about yourself. You can use these details as evidence when explaining the skills you have to offer as you apply for jobs.

Your activities are important to selectors, be they at work (managing the student union bar, sales experience in the summer holidays) or leisure (organising the Christmas party for the Biology Club). Analyse them for evidence of the skills mentioned above (see Figure 4 for an example). Keep this analysis in your career management file.

Academic activities can also show an employer you have much to offer that could be useful in the workplace (see Figure 5).

Other academic activities provide evidence
You can display evidence of skills and personal qualities in other areas of your course, such as:

Skill	Activity
planning	identifying where you want to go
budgeting	organising money
research	getting information
problem-solving	when problems arise
communication skills	using languages, meeting people, being sensitive to others
dealing with change	moving from one culture to another
evaluating	what I would have done differently, what I enjoyed, what I didn't
thinking ahead	plans for the next trip
energy, enthusiasm, initiative	you've done something extra in your holidays

Fig. 4. Skills acquired inter-railing.

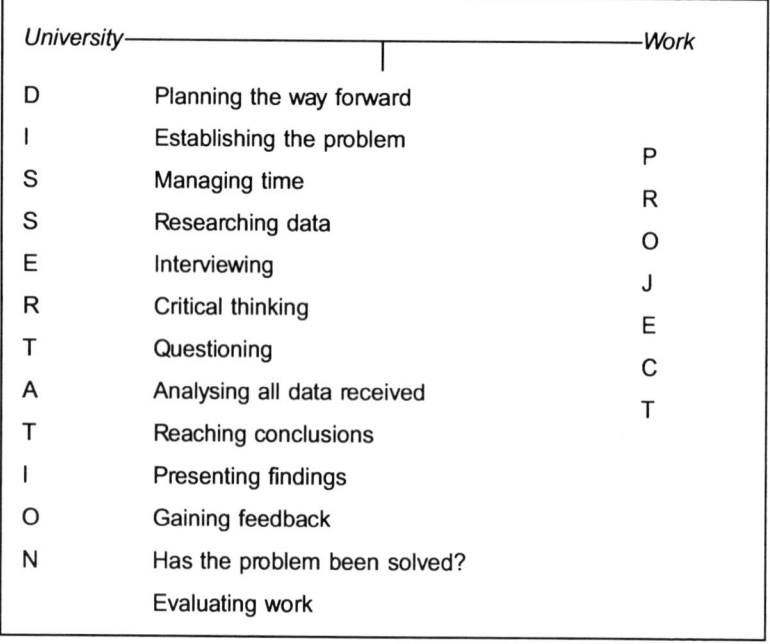

Fig. 5. Academic activities develop transferable skills.

- leading seminars
- giving presentations
- writing reports and essays
- attending lectures
- participating in group discussions
- undertaking lab work
- going on field trips.

Identify your strengths

Looking through your analysis, identify your strengths and weaknesses and rank them accordingly. Again, keep the ranking in your management file.

1 = This is a strong skill that I have
2 = I'm quite good at this
3 = I can do it but not brilliantly
4 = I can vaguely do this
5 = I do not have this skill

	1	2	3	4	5
Managing *Me* *Projects* *Change*					
Leading others					
Analysing					
Communicating					
Team working					
Solving problems					
Initiative and drive					
Planning and organising					
Receptive to learning					
Business awareness					

RELATING YOUR SKILLS AND INTERESTS TO JOBS

Extend the skills which interest and excite you.

Which skills do you want to use? Tick them:

Achieving results	Creating	Keeping records	Restoring
Advising	Designing	Listening	Researching
Administering	Diagnosing	Making	Selling
Analysing	Displaying	Managing	Servicing
Answering	Evaluating	Monitoring	Setting targets
Assembling	Finding solutions	Negotiating	Supervising
Assessing	Fund raising	Networking	Supporting
Budgeting	Guiding	Operating	Taking risks
Caring	Helping	Organising	Talking
Classifying	Identifying gaps	Persuading	Terminating
Coaching	Imagining	Planning	Training
Collecting	Implementing	Preparing	Watching
Comforting	Installing	Producing	Writing
Conserving	Interviewing	Programming	
Consulting	Inventing	Promoting	
Counselling	Investigating	Questioning	

List the skills you ticked in order of preference. Which ones would you like to use most of the day? and the least?

Many of the graduate positions do not require a particular discipline. Which of the following use the skills you've indicated you'd like to use?

Retail management	Banking	Police
Accountancy	Marketing	Actuary
Stockbroker	Sales	Public relations
Immigration	Systems analyst	Lecturing
Employment consultant	Voluntary organiser	Building society
Publican	Publishing	Investment analyst
Advertising	Charity fund raiser	Prison service
Local government	Applications programmer	Health & Safety
Teaching	Chartered secretary	inspector
Army	Airlines	Insurance
Human resources	Journalism	European Commission
Media sales	Inland Revenue	Self-employment
Royal Air Force	Personal assistant	Financial services
Computing	Careers officer	Transport manager
Administration	Social worker	Operational research
Personnel	Merchandising	Management
Treasurer	Distribution	consulting
Diplomatic Service	Information manager	

These jobs all need transferable skills, *eg* marketing and human resources management both require:

- managing self, others and projects
- communicating skills, working with clients and customers
- business awareness, strategic thinking, vision
- team member, working with others, in a variety of roles
- initiative, drive
- problem-solving, determination to overcome barriers and difficulties
- critical analysis skills, making sense of large amounts of information
- planning and organising, thinking ahead
- receptiveness to training, keeping in touch with a rapidly moving market.

Plus: computer literacy and numeracy skills; foreign languages will increase their options in the job place. They will need personal qualities such as commitment, motivation and resilience.

Taking this further
Look at relating your interests and skills to jobs by:

- talking to a careers adviser
- using computer-aided guidance software programmes, *eg* Gradscope, Adult Directions, Prospects
- looking carefully at advertisements for vacancies and the skills and qualities that are demanded. Do you have them?

Think broadly
Taking three of the jobs listed above, which sorts of companies might have vacancies in these areas?

Think long term
When you are thinking about future employment, remember that jobs come and go overnight. Your job might vanish, but you'll still have your skills and abilities to transfer to another area of work, combined with an ability to learn fast.

IDENTIFYING YOUR POTENTIAL

What is your potential?
This area can be looked at in several ways, such as:

Your ability and commitment to train for professional qualifications
If you are applying for a career where further training and qualifications will be necessary, an employer will want to know that:

- you can start and finish a course
- you have the ability to succeed – your exam results show you can.

Employers don't want to invest time and money training someone who lacks the commitment to complete the course. They know, however, that every course has its high and low moments so they may ask you to identify and evaluate which parts of your course were most difficult for you. How did you tackle them? How would you deal with similar difficulties at work?

Your potential to take on responsibility
How much responsibility can you handle and how soon? Employers will look for evidence of **leadership** and **management potential** if they require such abilities, including enthusiasm, the willingness to take responsibility and to go out and make things happen.

Look at your list of responsibilities and achievements and ask yourself:

- What motivates you to take responsibility?
- When you took on a responsibility, what did it involve? Did you want to take on more responsibility? If so, how much?
- How much responsibility do you like to have early on? Can you jump in at the deep end, grasp the situation and get it moving?
- How did you handle tasks in areas where you were not sure of what to do?

Your desire to reach the top
If you don't know what life is like at the top of an organisation, work shadow someone at that level for a week to find out. Some firms and university careers services operate work shadowing schemes, so check with your service.

Ask yourself:

- What qualities do you need to be a manager?
- Do you have them?
- If so, what evidence can you show that you have them?
- Is being at the top for you? If so, what appeals about it?

Adding value

Being able to offer the extras
Some employers want extra skills, knowledge and abilities from

candidates. They may include these as ways to eliminate applicants from a long list of people who have applied for a position.

Boost your skills base
Look at the suggested extras below. Can you offer evidence any of these skills?

Skill	*Example of evidence*
Numerate	GCSE Maths (B grade)
	GNVQ Advanced Level: Application of Number
Computer literate	Can use Word for Windows, Powerpoint, do spreadsheets, use computers for communication purposes
Foreign languages	GCSE French (C grade)
	Conversational German
Cultural awareness	Worked with people of different backgrounds and cultures as a sales assistant
	Inter-railing trip enhanced my awareness of different cultures
Knowledge of current affairs	Regular reader of *The Times* and the *Economist*
Driver	Clean driving licence

Getting some extra skills
These extras can increase your chances of getting a job – if you haven't got them, find out what is available in your area to boost your extras base. If you have left university and have not found a job, it can be a particularly useful activity: it will show an employer that you've used your time constructively while increasing your chances of getting work.

Identify ways to strengthen your weaknesses
How? Examples are:

- public speaking course to improve your presentation style and confidence

- computer literacy course to develop your strengths and understanding of IT.

ADDING YOUR PERSONAL TOUCH

To give an employer a rounded picture of your personality, identify your personal qualities and incorporate them into your CV, application form or covering letter. Tick the attributes listed below that you think describe you.

Kind	Caring	Good listener
Supportive	Assertive	Leader
Committed	Gentle	Questioner
Hard-worker	Numerate	Motivated
Sociable	Promoter	Punctual
Energetic	Enthusiastic	Disciplined
Doer	Quiet	Loud
Dedicated	Solitary	Innovator
Ideas person	Shy	Lots of stamina
Confident	Good natured	Patient
Quick thinker	Resilient	Controlled
Cautious	Self-confident	Independent
Persistent	Need support	Decisive
Quick tempered	Quick learner	Resourceful

INCREASING YOUR KNOWLEDGE BASE

- Add to your self-knowledge by talking to friends and family whom you trust, especially if they are in work: they will be well placed to see how your qualities relate to employment.

- Discuss your skills base with your fellow students: exchanging ideas will expand your thoughts on the subject.

- Attend introduction to management courses designed to give you an insight into management if your university offers them.

- You will always need a good knowledge of your strengths and skills so that you can market yourself well to an employer.

- Most activities at work have a strong team focus and so employers want to recruit people who will fit in and work as part of a team. An applicant with the right qualifications won't necessarily 'fit' socially.

CASE STUDIES

Sarah takes stock of her plans

Sarah's tutor group met with the personnel team at a local bank. The personnel manager explained that, when recruiting, they looked for people who had 'gone out and done things, who've got an ability to achieve'. At home, Sarah pushed aside her project and tentatively wrote down her achievements. 'Getting to my first choice of university,' she wrote, 'market research – company pleased with the results, chosen to be Ophelia in play, organised visit by acting group'. As Sarah continued listing her achievements and activities, she started to feel more positive. Now she had something to show about herself, she booked an appointment with the careers adviser.

Matthew is looking at the wrong job

Matthew knew the skills he enjoyed using: promoting, communicating, working with people, solving problems, negotiating, researching. At the careers service, he booked in to have a session on Prospects, a computer-aided guidance programme. To his surprise, Public Relations Officer appeared. With the help of a careers officer, Matthew analysed the skills and strengths he enjoyed using. He started to realise perhaps accountancy wasn't for him. 'Why were you so keen on accountancy?' asked the careers officer. 'Well, I've spent a lot of time in accountants' firms so it seemed the logical thing to do,' Matthew replied. 'But perhaps I need to take a fresh look at my career prospects.'

Mary looks through her skills

Mary had a reputation among her friends as a good listener. She wanted to get work as a counsellor, helping people solve their problems. While she had been at university, it had been impossible for her to join any voluntary help lines – Mary had been too busy looking after the family and studying. Now that she had finished her degree, however, Mary wanted to devote time to helping people in need. She signed up as a volunteer with the Samaritans and underwent their training programme.

DISCUSSION POINTS

1. Why do people go to university? What were your reasons for going?

2. What can you offer an employer over someone who has not been to university or college? What are the advantages of employing someone who is 21 or 22 rather than 18?

3. What value have you added to your CV since you started higher education?

3
Getting in Touch with Reality

GETTING IN TOUCH WITH WORK

A nervous workforce
Quality assurance, downsizing, accountability, customer care, technological developments, international developments and competitiveness have all made the workplace a much tougher, more frantic, exciting and exhausting environment. Managers, researchers and product developers, sales and marketing staff, administrators and clerks are all under pressure as a result. People in work have twice the workload they had previously. The stakes are higher and the rewards greater – but it's a turbulent, nervous ride. Redundancy is common to make way for a streamlined, cost-effective workforce. Many employees are nervous as a result.

Skills and personal qualities are a must
There is an increased demand for managers, administrators, workers in the service sector such as retail, leisure, tourism and the hospitality industry; and within the professional areas, including law, education and health. Support services are needed via financial services and information technology. These areas demand an aptitude for working with colleagues and customers and providing a high standard of service to both.

You can work in most places
The world is a smaller place, thanks to technological advances, and this means that it's harder to get away from work – for example, when you get home, days off, holidays, working away. The office can always reach you. Plus people expect a faster response to letters, memos, questions, queries, and requests, because the technology means that rapid answers can be given. People who don't keep up with change are most likely to lose out in the job market.

However, it is easier to work across borders, thanks to technological developments, involving transport, communications and engineering, political changes and the media. You can work from anywhere when you have a telephone, fax, PC, Internet *etc.*

A flexible workforce is essential
So a wide range of ways to be employed has developed including:

- home-based workers
- part-time work, *eg* three days a week, four days, two days, 15 hours a week
- consultants
- temps
- contract workers, *eg* for six, nine or twelve months
- career breaks, *eg* for up to five years
- locals abroad if labour costs are cheaper to reduce costs.

You could combine some of these methods and find yourself working full time.

International competition demands the best
Many organisations are trying to produce world class products at cost-effective prices, so naturally they want to recruit the best people. Many employers have become much more **results orientated**, where employees are expected to exceed targets. Hence they need people who have already proven themselves to be achievers.

Bringing out the best in people
Organisations and countries are trying to make the most of their most valuable resource – people – and as a result a wide variety of careers has developed:

Private trainers	Personnel officers
Trainers in colleges of further education	Careers consultants
Trainers in specialist colleges	Careers advisers
Training consultants	Careers teachers
One-to-one trainers	Human resource directors
Training advisers	Recruitment consultants
Outplacement specialists	Researchers
Training writers	Government advisers
Trainers in the public sector	Management trainers
Training managers	Management consultants

Speed is of the essence
IT and communications developments mean that there are many avenues for job hunting such as the Internet (see Chapter 6) in addition

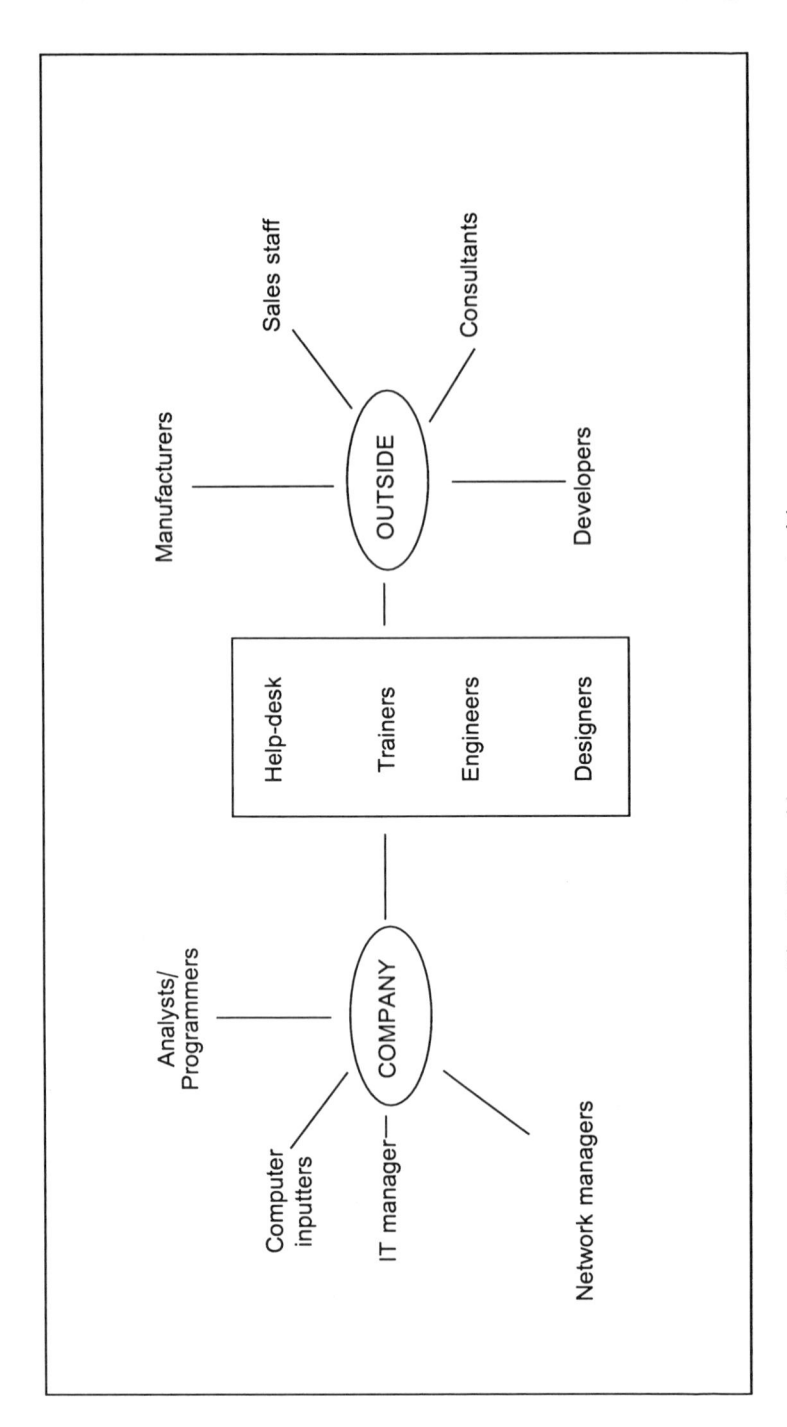

Fig. 6. IT provides many careers opportunities.

to the many opportunities in the field of information technology itself (see Figure 6).

Re-skilling can be a necessity
The economic landscape has changed dramatically recently as old industries (coal and steel) and agriculture have been replaced or displaced with new hi-tech areas and service industries. Unskilled or low skilled work is rapidly disappearing. Career opportunities are increasing in professional, managerial, technical and skilled areas, hence employers want to recruit people with the relevant abilities and interpersonal skills to offer or the potential to develop them. Continuous training and learning is a vital tool to keep up with change in technology and opportunities in employment.

Increased career choice
As technology has advanced, a new range of careers has developed, *eg* the media, television, documentaries, films, journalism, radio, photography, screen-writing, advertising, public relations, satellite systems.

Growing career areas
- retail
- charity organisations (fund-raisers, promoters)
- hospitality and leisure sector
- health and social work, community service work, education, training
- recruitment
- technology, computing, electrical goods
- media and media sales.

Shrinking career opportunities
- public administration and defence
- construction, energy and water supply
- transport, storage and communication
- agriculture, forestry and fishing
- mining and quarrying.

(Source: *Financial Mail*, December 1995)

There is, however, a wide variety of opportunities for graduates in some of these areas, such as the finance industry.

Graduates go into a variety of careers, including:

Accounting	Voluntary work	Engineering
Education	Recruitment	International relations
Personnel	Leisure industry	Manufacturing
Law	Temporary work	Retail
Local government	Travel industry	Public services
Training	Energy industries	Consultancy based work
Media	Finance	Secretarial/Personal assistant
Pharmaceutical	Construction industry	Marketing

FINDING WHERE YOU FIT IN

Looking at trends
In the old days
Years ago, the stay-on rate in post-16 education was much lower. It didn't necessarily matter, because there was lots of unskilled or low-skilled work for school-leavers to go into and people learned on the job as apprentices, often taught by a supervisor. Graduates formed a tiny percentage of the population – few jobs required highly skilled, intellectually capable people.

In the 1990s things are different
Young people aged 16 have been encouraged to stay on in education, partly to increase their chances and flexibility in the job market, but also because unskilled and low-skilled jobs are disappearing and employers need people who could be immediately effective in the workplace (*ie* who needed no basic training). The routes into higher education opened up considerably to encourage more people to take the opportunity to attend university or college and gain a higher level of qualification.

In the meantime, a **global economy** had developed, thereby heightening international competition and introducing the 'world class' theory, whereby companies needed the very best if they were to compete and stay ahead. Advances in technology meant that low-skilled jobs were vanishing: employers needed people who could supervise and monitor machinery, undertake research and development (to keep them ahead in new products). They wanted recruits with fine interpersonal skills, the ability to handle increasingly complex amounts of information and systems, to cope with change, pressure and – in short – anything that was thrown at them. Hence work experience gives people an immediate strategic advantage: they can get stuck in and make an impact more quickly so saving many companies time and money.

Bang went the rules
There are no rules any more. The routes to qualify and succeed are

more varied now. More people are taking time out, short-term projects, part-time work, consultancy, freelance as the workplace becomes more fractured. Drive, determination and a desire and passion to make things happen are central to the workforce

Every single employee counts
Employers have to make the most of all people at work, not just graduates – every single member of staff is invaluable and can make an impact. Responsibility at work has been downloaded – especially as middle management have been eroded as a group. Many jobs have changed dramatically, such as secretarial and personal assistants. No more are they expected to spend their working days typing letters and making tea: now many managers do their own letters as they have the technology and the secretary has thus been freed up to do other things and take on more responsibility.

Getting that first job!
Initially, your competition for work may include:

- your fellow graduates
- previous graduates who took a year off or decided to move organisations
- people already in work who have progressed through the ranks at work, acquiring professional qualifications and having the right attitude
- continentals, recruited for their language abilities
- a mixture of 18-year-olds leaving school/college, mature entrants and graduates.

UNDERSTANDING YOUR OPTIONS IN WORK

Traditional routes to work
Tried and tested routes to work after graduation include:

- graduate trainee scheme, *eg* retail
- professional training, *eg* accountancy
- specific job with individual training negotiated with firm by you
- post-graduate study – vocational or research
- trainee scheme not requiring degree as such but your skills and qualities.

Non-traditional routes into work
These include the following:

Own business   Temping – as a career or short term
Network marketing   Short-term job with a specific goal in mind
Portfolio worker   Short training course with goal in mind
Franchise operator

This means there are more ways to find your route into a job.

Employers' needs change
Employers have different needs and many will try to align recruitment programmes with current and forecasted developments within the business, so graduate opportunities will inevitably change. Increasingly, many firms are recruiting as the need arises, rather than at a specific time of the year.

Methods of recruiting differ
Large companies are more likely to have a personnel (and training) department, and even graduate recruitment managers. Their recruitment processes may take some time and will invariably involve advertising for vacancies, application forms and assessment centres. Smaller companies are more likely to recruit as and when they need staff – the faster the process the more cost-effective it is for them.

YOU'VE GOT MORE CHOICE

Your career path is likely to look very different now from perhaps your grandparents' choices when they left school.

From little choice...
In the past, there was less career choice than there is today. For example, girls chose between nursing, secretarial work or teaching before getting married and having children. Most lives followed the pattern in Figure 7.

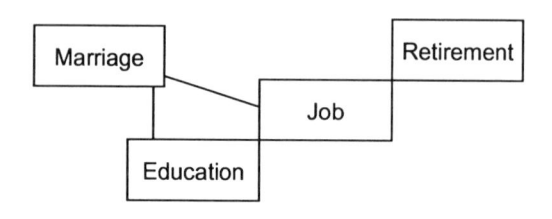

Fig. 7. Original career choice.

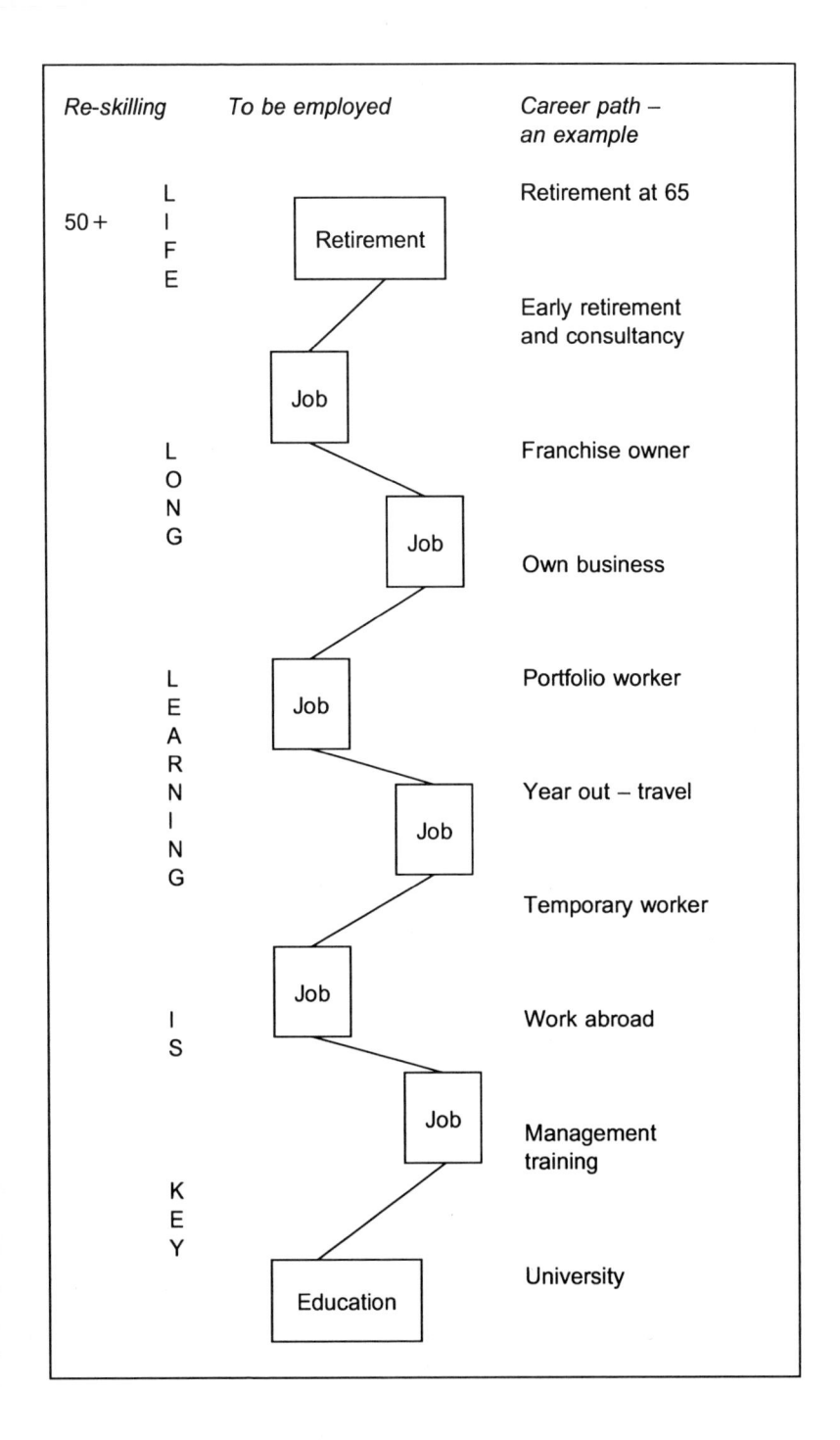

Re-skilling	To be employed	Career path – an example
50+	L I F E	Retirement at 65
	Retirement	
		Early retirement and consultancy
	Job	
		Franchise owner
L O N G	Job	Own business
L E A R N I N G	Job	Portfolio worker
	Job	Year out – travel
		Temporary worker
	Job	
I S		Work abroad
	Job	Management training
K E Y	Education	University

Fig. 8. The way forward looks different now.

...To a jungle of choice
Compare Figure 7 with Figure 8.

This is just one example of having a satisfying career, building up blocks of skills and experience which are all transferable. You could still remain with one company throughout your career, but those now at the top of organisations tend to be between the ages of 39 and 45, with experience of several companies plus a stint working abroad.

Making your way forward
How you cut your path through the jungle is entirely up to you. It depends what you want to find on the other side.

DON'T FORGET SMALL FIRMS!

They're big business!
Small and medium sized firms are **big employers**. Businesses with fewer than 100 people form half of the UK non-government workforce according to *Labour Market Trends* (December 1995) so don't ignore them in your job hunting. Smaller employers are even less likely to have time to keep up with educational changes so you will need to be explicit about what your degree covers. They don't have time or money to go through the entire application process. Enlisting the help of outside agencies means a lot of the work is done for them. They will be interested in your skills and your ability to get stuck in and contribute rapidly to the workplace. They can be friendly, lively places to work and you may have more opportunity to contribute quickly to business strategies.

Finding them
- Check with your local TEC – it should have a good knowledge of local businesses.
- *Yellow Pages* in local telephone directories (usually available in local libraries).
- For live vacancies, try recruitment agencies, PeopleBank or JobSite.

What line of work are they in?
According to the DTI, small firms are in areas such as computer software, advertising and business services, entertainment, sport and catering, real estate, road transport, vehicle maintenance and repair.

Getting in Touch with Reality

Questions and answers

What sorts of things do I need to find out about the job market in my career area of choice?
Find out information such as:
- What is the job market likely to be in the future?
- What range of organisations can you work for?
- What is the scope for setting up on your own?
- What are the recent and future changes in the field?
- What are the international opportunities?

Where can I find out what past graduates have done both from my university and nationwide?
Your university careers service should have destination statistics for all its students. There will always be some who cannot be tracked for various reasons. Some departments also like to track past graduates to show newcomers what their past students have done. For an idea of what graduates do nationwide, try *What do Graduates do?* an annual publication by CRAC.

SUMMARY

- The more informed you are about the employment market as a whole, the better placed you will be to find your niche.
- This will always give you the edge over others!
- Many employers recruit throughout the year as the need arises.

CASE STUDIES

Sarah starts her research
Sarah bought a copy of the local paper. To her surprise, she found herself turning to the recruitment pages first of all. She was excited by the range of vacancies and started to wonder what the job situation was like back home. From being really scared about her future, Sarah started to feel excited. She knew she had something to offer, which had increased her confidence tenfold.

Matthew sets a strategy
Matthew had been so set on accountancy he felt quite lost now that he realised it was not for him. He dreaded ringing his father to tell him about his change of heart – he was a partner in a senior accountancy firm. 'I'll do more research before I call,' Matthew thought. He started reading the papers to learn about employment patterns and trends and

to see what skills and abilities employers wanted.

Mary reads the local papers for hints

Mary had already contacted the relevant local departments to see what services they offered and she decided to try to spend some time in each to find out which one would suit her the most. However, she was intrigued to read in the local paper one night that there was to be a new counselling service set up for young people. Mary picked up the phone and spoke to the lady in charge of recruitment. 'May I come in and talk to you about it?' she asked. 'I'm currently studying for a degree which has a strong counselling element in it, specifically geared to young people and I'd love to be a part of the new service.' An appointment was made for Mary to get further information.

DISCUSSION POINTS

1. Who should pay for training? The government? Employers? Employees? All three? Why?

2. How might work change in the future?

3. What is work?

4
Establishing your Needs and Values

DEFINING HAPPINESS AND SUCCESS

People have different views of success and happiness. To achieve a 'successful career', you need to decide how your personal and career goals are interlinked.

Laura wants the freedom to do as she pleases
'I graduated in graphic design,' Laura says. 'Friends say I should start my own business, but I don't want the pressure. Temping's great. I work when I want and take weeks off to go skiing. I can turn up at an office at 9.00 and leave at 5.00.'

Mike is driven to succeed
'I work in the City,' Mike says. 'The hours are long and the pressure is immense, but I love it. My goal is to make a million as soon as I can and set up my own business.'

Both Laura and Mike are happy because they know what they want for now. Laura wants the freedom to do as she pleases, whereas Mike is working towards his own goals. Does this change?

Laura goes on the career path
Laura went temping for a year but she became bored: she wanted more responsibility. Busy friends in graphic design were constantly asking her to work for them on a freelance basis. Laura reduced her temping to two weeks a month, and spent the other two weeks freelancing. By the end of the year, she was freelancing full time. 'I just needed a break after all that work at college,' she reflects.

Mike burns out and seeks a change
Mike loved his job in the City with its financial rewards. After three years, however, he started to feel unhappy. Talking to old university friends, Mike realised he only had his job to talk about. His life *was* his

job. He booked a week's holiday, reassessed his goals and decided to give his job another 12 months before spending a year travelling.

What do success and happiness mean to you?
Identify your meaning of success and happiness (tick appropriately):

Good balance of work and outside interests	_____
Job satisfaction	_____
Recognition for what you do at work	_____
Good job prospects	_____
Comfortable living style	_____
Ability to go on the sort of holidays you want	_____
That car you've always wanted	_____
Your own home	_____
Having a family	_____
Ability to pursue your hobbies and interests regularly	_____
The chance to face regular new challenges (not necessarily at work)	_____
Financial security in the future	_____
A job you love	_____
Respected in the community	_____
Making a contribution to the world	_____
Other (name it):	_____

Try to incorporate your definitions of happiness and success into your career planning.

Question and answer
My partner and I met at university. I'm worried about what will happen after this year. We want to stay together – but how can we in a climate of so much change?
You need to talk about this together. Work out what you want from life. Are your values and needs the same? You may need to compromise in some areas (both of you) and you should revisit your goals and

values regularly, because you will both change just as circumstances do. Plan your futures together and share your goals. Revisit your plans regularly.

HOW FAR DO YOU WANT TO GO?

There are many ways to progress your career, namely moving:

- up
- sideways, *ie* doing a different job at the same level with different responsibilities
- abroad
- between organisations
- to work for yourself.

Staying with one firm
Do you want to move up with one organisation or would you prefer to change to progress? Check with prospective companies to see what their policy is in promoting people – do they promote internally or recruit from outside?

Qualifying for promotion
Further qualifications may help. You could look at gaining them on a part-time basis, *eg* working for an NVQ in management, or studying for an MBA (usually you need business experience first), or registering to do a PhD at a local university on a part-time basis. Professional qualifications, *eg* medicine, law, accountancy, recruitment consulting or banking, may be a must if you are to practise.

Moving organisations
People change organisations more frequently now. Some companies advertise for graduates who've had a couple of years out of university and acquired experience and been successful – but who are looking for a move. You'll find out a lot about yourself and what you want out of work through being in work.

The pros of moving up
- more money
- greater contribution to company strategy
- more perks
- greater satisfaction.

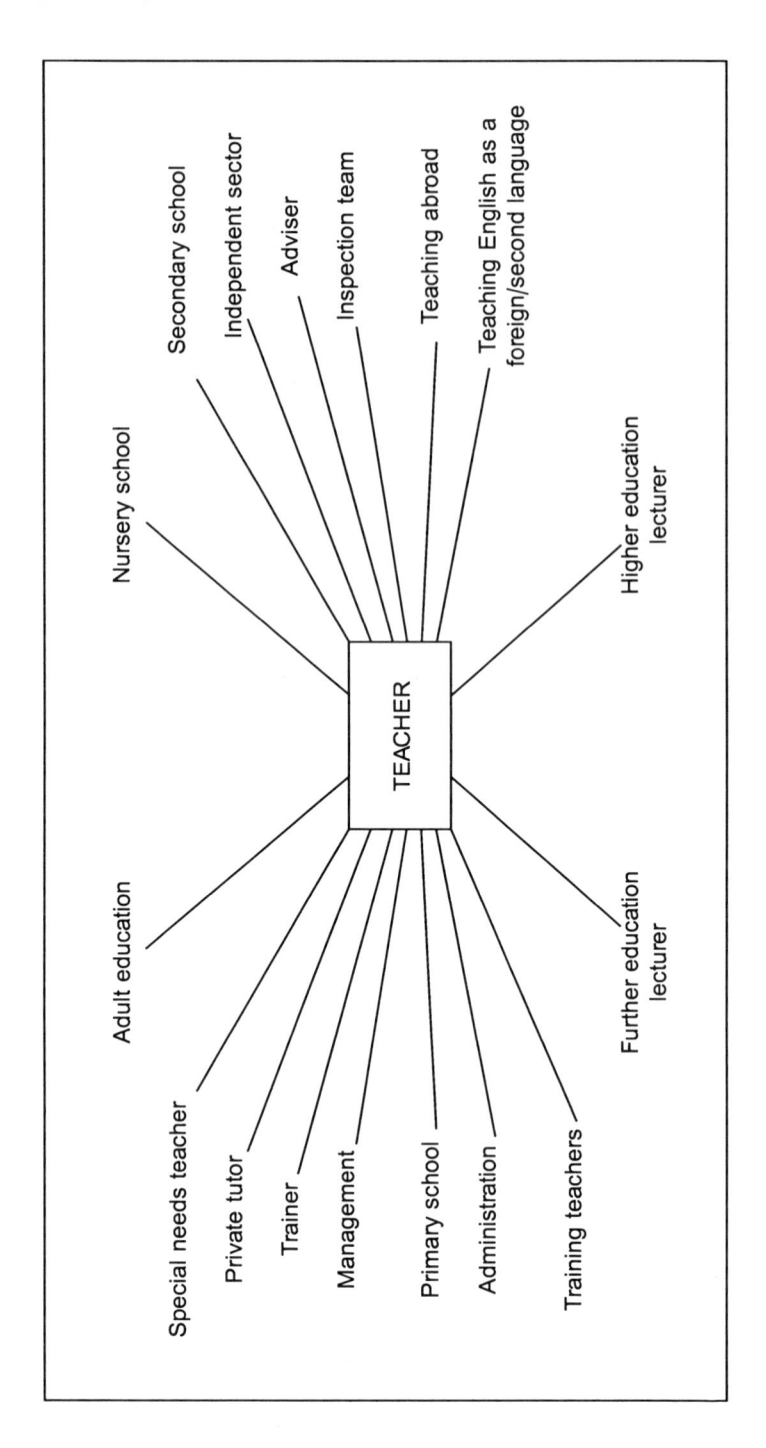

Fig. 9. Specialising.

Establishing your Needs and Values

And the cons
- you may move away from what you were originally trained to do as management of others, contribution to strategy, involvement in budgeting, public relations and client liaison take more of your time
- increased responsibility means that you may take work home with you and that your work follows you everywhere
- it may be harder to keep in touch at the grass roots level, *eg* headteachers often miss teaching

Do you want to specialise?
Do you want to be a **specialist** or a **generalist**? Specialists know a great deal about their subject and may often be called in as consultants or advisers on special features. For example, if you decide to train as a teacher, there are a whole host of things you could do in teaching as specialisms – see Figure 9.

Generalists have a broader outlook, for example 'General Manager' as opposed to 'IT Manager'.

Do you want to play a major role in
an organisation's direction? _____

Do you want to be responsible for others? _____

How far do you want to specialise? _____

THINKING ABOUT SIZE AND LOCATION

How large?
What size of company would you like to work for? Weigh up the pros and cons of working for a small and large company:

Small companies	*Large companies*
Less bureaucracy	Hierarchical structures
Fewer chances for promotion	More chances of promotion
Less likely to have structured training programme	Could be training and policy adviser
Lots of variety – all hands on deck	Less variety – jobs more specialised
Real team effort	Difficulties of communication

Less likely to have social club but friendly atmosphere makes up

Social/sports club – but feeling of not knowing others in the organisation

May have more of a valued feeling

Could provide opportunities for work on a long-term basis

Where do you want to work?
- in your home town?
- in your university town?
- abroad?
- city, town, countryside?
- commuter belt?

Think about:
- accommodation costs
- getting to work, *ie* cost and length of journey from your house/flat/bed-sit
- moving to where the jobs are, *ie* those areas with higher employment levels.

You may decide that location doesn't matter; although if you get a job offer in Inverness and your partner is going to Truro, you may need to think again.

Be prepared to move if you can
This is easier if you are free from commitments such as family *etc*. If you can, think about moving to areas where there is a good record of employment. Unemployment levels vary from region to region so keep an eye on papers to see which areas look good. You can always move later on.

Your preferred region/city to work in is: _____

Which size of organisation do you prefer? _____

LEARNING MORE

A degree isn't enough on its own
The good news is that all this studying has taught you how to learn. The bad news (for some readers) is that learning is now a continual, life-long process.

Training to be effective at work

Companies train employees in order to make the most effective use of their most valuable resource: people. Carefully thought out training programmes may be delivered to meet a need that has been identified. An effective training programme should enable employees to enhance their performance and thereby offer a higher quality service (and product) to their clientele. These courses may last one or two days, *eg* 'Giving performance appraisals at work'.

Some companies invest heavily in training. Others don't, possibly because they do not have the resources or because they believe in learning on the job – 'the way I did it'. When you are considering prospective employers, look at their training structure and ask about the support for training.

Training for the future

Your employer may train you to do your job more effectively, but not necessarily to cater for your future career development. (He may worry that you'll leave after he's forked out for courses for you.) Training for further qualifications will increase your flexibility in the job market so investigate further opportunities.

Questions and answers

Have I got the stamina to cope with training? How much time and effort do I want to commit to working for professional qualifications?
This requires serious deliberation, especially if you are thinking about qualifying for a profession. Ask trainees about their working day and see if it is going to suit you, *eg* are you prepared to work an eight-hour day in the office then go home at night and put in another two or three hours' work? 'If you're not prepared to put this sort of time in, then don't think about becoming an accountant,' says one weary trainee.

I want a rest from studying and working for qualifications. I've had enough – it's been non-stop ever since I started school. I don't want to train – I just want a job where I don't have to worry about more studying. I'm tired of it. Can I just work and not bother about training?
Training increases your flexibility in the job market, improves your effectiveness at work, and may be essential in order to qualify for membership of some professional bodies. Your degree has taught you how to learn, but you can't rest on it. Keep learning and training and you're move likely to survive and do well in the job market.

Evaluate your thoughts on training
- Do you want to train merely for the job you are doing?
- Or for a professional qualification?
- What are your preferred learning methods?
- How much training do you want?
- What do you want to gain from it?

TAKE FIVE: GIVE ME A BREAK!

'I want to take time out – perhaps temp and travel – then look for a job,' says Simone, a geography student. 'I want to have a rest from full-time education and do something different before I settle down to work.'

Many students choose to do this. Some employers encourage it. 'Gets it out of their system,' is a commonly heard phrase. Check Chapter 9 for ways to get short-term work.

Whatever your plans, make sure that:

- your year out is constructive
- it will add currency to your CV
- you think and plan ahead so that you can build up the right skills and experience for your future career and plug any missing gaps.

Are you looking for a job or a career?
A job is usually short term:

- a task you perform at work as part of your career
- a position you apply for on a short-term basis as a stop gap – 'I'll do this job for six months, then travel'
- vacation employment.

Pros of having a job
- it can be a way of gaining experience to add to your CV, *eg* volunteering for a task at work that's extra to your responsibilities
- it can provide you with money and pay off debts
- it can fit in to short-term plans
- it can be very temporary.

Cons of having a job
- it may not challenge you
- it might be underpaid.

Do you want a short-term job to meet
a goal or a serious career move?   _____

What do you want to achieve from them?   _____

A chance to work abroad

Many people want to work abroad and there are many ways to fulfil this dream:

- Find a job in the country you wish to go to and do it all independently.
- Use agencies and colleges which train people for specific jobs and then help them find work through their networks, *eg* teaching English abroad.
- Do voluntary work abroad.
- Work for organisations where the nature of the work takes you abroad, *eg* the forces, the European Commission (competitive).
- Take your career abroad, *eg* to nurse, teach, promote health.
- Work for international organisations which have offices all over the world (*ie* aim to get transferred).
- Work for firms where your language capabilities or vocational experience take you abroad on projects or visits for brief periods.
- Have a UK-based job involving a lot of international travel.

Which countries would you prefer to work in?   _____

Preferred method of working abroad: _____
(*eg* as indicated above)

EARNING MONEY

How important is the money you earn? Some people would prefer to have a very interesting job from which they derive great satisfaction with less pay, than an incredibly boring job which pays them very well. Most of us want both the satisfying job and the money.
Ask yourself:

- What is the starting salary – but what could it be in say five years' time? ten years? fifteen?

Free or subsidised travel costs	Overtime pay
Free or subsidised home telephone	Luncheon vouchers
Private health insurance	Season ticket loans
Private pension	Training
Mortgage assistance	Company car
Bonuses	Relocation costs
Holidays	Flexitime
Free parking	Free or subsidised meals
Free or subsidised accommodation	Free banking
Gym membership	Social club

Fig. 10. Examples of perks.

Establishing your Needs and Values

- What factors are likely to influence the amount you get (*eg* state/private sector, area you live in, working abroad, the type of organisation)?
- Do you want a company where bonuses relate to your performance, *ie* if you do a job really well, you get a bigger bonus?
- Do you want to have access to a profit-sharing scheme, *ie* if the whole company does well, you gain financially?

GET will give you a good idea of starting salaries, but you should consider the whole package you are offered, for example, perks can be invaluable especially if they take your long-term future into account.

Being perky... any extras?
Some companies offer a range of perks to staff, which can add greatly to the value of the package offered (see Figure 10). In times of recession, these may disappear. There may be disadvantages to some perks: for example, they may not be free. Your company will declare any perks you do get to the tax man.

Thinking about your non-financial values
If you're researching prospective employers, think about:

- location
- size of organisation
- atmosphere
- likely hours
- the culture, *eg* formal (Good morning, Mr Smith) or informal (Morning, Jim).

BEING INDEPENDENT

Do you want to work for yourself?
- Have you got an entrepreneurial spirit? Can you identify new business opportunities?
- Do you want to succeed?
- Have you got readily identified skills and ideas you could use in a business?
- Do you like taking risks?
- Can you manage: take responsibility, make decisions, plan ahead?

- Can you sell things, win customers over?
- Are you willing to work long hours?
- Can you deal with the administration and routine matters of business?
- Can you solve problems?
- Can you think of ideas that might make a business?

When starting a business, you need to think about:
- the aim of your business
- who your clients could be
- what services or products you will sell and how you will fight off any competition
- what the start up costs will be and how you would pay for them
- what facilities you would need and how you would acquire them.

Get information on self-employment from:
- banks (special advisers available to talk to people who want to run their own businesses)
- LiveWIRE can put you in touch with a local business link (see Useful Addresses)
- your local TEC
- your university careers service: it may run sessions on starting your own business.

You could be a portfolio worker
Portfolio workers have two or three jobs. For example, Jane teaches adults Spanish and sells books through network marketing.

Network marketing
Create your own job working from home through **network marketing**, *eg* selling books, make-up, household products *etc* for a company. You purchase a start-up pack and usually have the help of an adviser who can train you in the art of network marketing. A small amount of capital is required to start up – anything from £50 plus. You get as involved as you want to. Some people run a network marketing business while they have another job, until their 'day' job is taken over by the 'evening' one which becomes a full-time proposition. You could

start while you are studying for your degree! You create your own chain, by introducing friends and customers to the business.

Buying a franchise
This usually involves more capital and you may be required to have considerable business experience before buying in. You have the assurance of selling a well-known product, backed by people who have been involved in the business for some time. An example is the Body Shop.

Do you want to work for yourself?   YES/NO

Not now, maybe later   YES/NO

How much later?

CASE STUDIES

Sarah makes her first move.
'Are you going to stay in the area, then?' Sarah's friend Marion had noticed that she was looking through the jobs columns with great interest. 'I don't know,' Sarah said. 'But I should decide whether I want to, I suppose. Where would I live though?' Lecture over, Sarah and Marion wandered back to the student housing. 'It wouldn't be the same, being here while everyone else has gone,' Sarah reflected. 'Probably best to move. I could start looking back home, just something temporary while I'm really looking for something proper.'

Matthew looks at his values
Matthew realised that what was important to him was interest in the job, rather than money. 'You only live once,' his friend Tom told him. 'So enjoy it.' Tom was off to manage a fish farm in Scotland – he was doing agriculture and fish science. Matthew decided he wanted to move to a new town and start afresh. But he did want a job with prospects and training, preferably with qualifications, where he could be fairly independent. Matthew wanted a 'people' job where he could use his communication skills.

Mary needs to stay at home
Mary knew what she wanted: she needed to stay in the locality, she wanted to train further and wanted a job which would fit in with the hours she had available. The new counselling service offered all those, except the last one. 'You'd be needed here three days a week from 4.00

to 7.00,' she was told. 'Damn,' Mary thought, those are just the very hours I don't want to work. I need to be able to give that time to my own children. Mary had to look at other options.

DISCUSSION POINTS

1. Why do people work?

2. What impact has the European Union had on employment opportunities?

3. Should employers recruit nationals over foreigners, even if someone from abroad is better suited to the post?

5
Showing the Right Attitude and Image

ACQUIRING THE RIGHT ATTITUDE

You can have lots of qualifications, but if you aren't motivated and don't have the right attitude, it will be difficult to get a job. When people are sacked, it is often because they don't have the right attitude rather than because they lack the right qualifications and skills.

First impressions count

Everyone you meet in an organisation notices you, whether you are on work experience, work shadowing, interview days or an employer visit. Staff pay great attention to your attitude, appearance, manners, professionalism and enthusiasm. 'Will she fit in?' they'll wonder, and 'What will he be like to work with? Will he pull his weight?' They will notice your time-keeping, reliability and energy levels. Staff at all levels may be asked about you, especially if you're attending a job interview. After all, one day they may even have to work with you.

Going the extra mile

Employers look for evidence that you've gone out and done something extra because that's what they'll want you to do when you join them. They want people who can make a difference and make things happen.

Making things happen
This means to be a self-starter, to innovate, to provide solutions, to seek new customers, to begin a project and see it through, to put a strategy together and implement it. Have you got the drive, motivation and commitment to achieve?

It can be exciting, exhausting and rewarding
Demands on organisations are such that you will frequently do (probably unpaid) overtime to get things done. This may include working at the weekends.

Working with thought for others
Do you offer to make coffee/tea for others if you're doing it for yourself? Do you offer to help them if you've finished your work and can see they are busy? Small actions go a long way in creating a happy atmosphere in the office and making people appreciate you.

Making customers feel special
Companies are increasingly trying to attract and retain customers through outstanding customer care and services. An example is the battle between British Airways and Virgin Atlantic, both fighting for custom on a valuable route. Custom cannot be won merely on extra facilities, for these mean nothing if they are not accompanied by the personal touch to make customers feel they are special. It is the total customer proposition that counts!

Professionalism, a desire for excellence and to be the BEST!
Today, people expect to receive and to purchase quality assured products. Customers are more likely to be well travelled and better educated; global economies have influenced this trend. In the quest for excellence, companies want to better their performance, and methods such as benchmarking, the process whereby companies measure their performance alongside proven indicators of success, have become common.

Don't moan and groan
Offices don't want people with a chip on their shoulder, who do not take responsibility and blame others for any problems, or who are no fun to work with. Don't whinge about past problems and complain about the graduate employment market or the tutor who didn't like you – you'll set hackles rising and irritate people in the office.

HOW HEALTHY IS YOUR ATTITUDE?

Employers want to recruit the very best
This applies at all levels. Organisations want to take on the finest people they can. They want people who can show a passion for the things they get involved in, people who have that sparkle and extra energy, who put that little bit of extra something into their activities. 'If the quality isn't there, we don't recruit,' is commonly heard through recruitment markets. If you're competing in a global economy, you have to produce a world class product. If you going to produce a world class product, you need the best people.

Showing the Right Attitude and Image

For many employers, the right sort of attitude and interpersonal skills are as important as qualifications – some would say more so. As the economy has become more service orientated with more emphasis on handling people (clients and staff), so these qualities are more crucial in the battle to be the best.

So what about you? Which of the following attributes reflect your attitude? Can you provide an example for each one?

Willing to go the extra mile   _____

Keen to take responsibility   _____

Having a positive attitude   _____

Wanting to do the best job you can   _____

Looking for ways to do that job even better   _____

Do you like to volunteer your help?   _____

Strong work commitment   _____

Caring about your organisation's image   _____

Pride in your achievements   _____

The customer comes first   _____

A passion for excellence   _____

Willingness to help colleagues   _____

Thoughtful about the way you deal with people   _____

Can you be relied on?   _____

HELPING YOURSELF

If you really are committed to getting a job, then you will need to:

- spend time looking for work
- be proactive and get out to look for the right job.

Can you suggest a way to find a job with a company that will get me ahead of the competition?
Writing on spec shows initiative and interest, but you should gear your cover letter to the employer you are writing to, so that he doesn't get a photocopy letter which has clearly been sent out to hundreds of other people. An action plan could be as shown in Figure 11.

Action

↓

Identify your skills, interest and values

↓

Research areas of employment that interest you

↓

Get a short list of prospective employers to contact

↓

Contact the right person in the organisation

↓

Arrange a meeting

↙ ↓ ↘

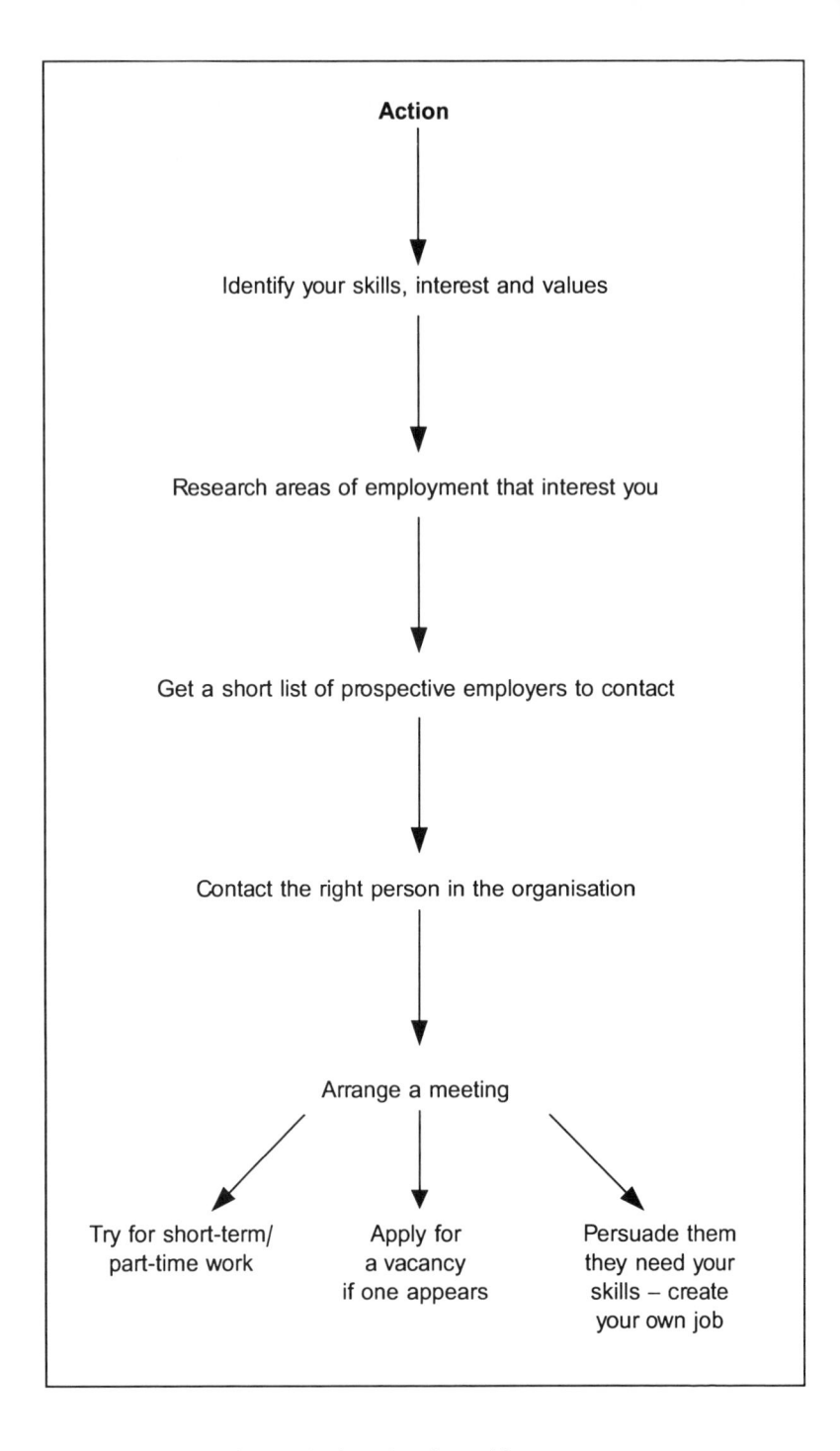

Try for short-term/part-time work | Apply for a vacancy if one appears | Persuade them they need your skills – create your own job

Fig. 11. Action plan for writing on spec.

Showing the Right Attitude and Image

THINKING ABOUT YOUR IMAGE

Your **image** will go a long way to helping you secure a job. Your image says a lot about you. It shows whether you care about the way others perceive you. Like it or not, many jobs are gained because a candidate made a visual impact and portrayed the right sort of image. 'We're not so concerned with what employees wear to work,' says one personnel director. 'But our customers are. A sloppy image makes the organisation look sloppy too.'

Meeting people

Remember that people you meet from the workplace could help you find a job. So when you go into work, look **professional**. You're going to work, not to a fashion show or on a date.

Tips to remember

- Check you have the correct names of those you are about to meet – including title and pronunciation.

- Sit only when asked to do so: 'Please, take a seat'.

- Don't call employers by their first names (*eg* Jackie, Mike) unless they tell you it is all right to do so.

- If you are in a discussion with a staff member and someone enters the room, stand up as a sign of respect and be prepared to be introduced (it could be the boss).

- Make sure it is all right for you to take notes.

- When you are sitting down, leaning forward very slightly indicates that you are paying great attention.

- Don't remove your jacket until the employer does and gives you permission to remove yours.

- Make 'I am listening' signs: nodding your head, saying 'yes' at intervals.

- Don't interrupt.

- Don't fear silence. If you need time to think about an answer, say so.

- Don't try to read papers on the desk in front of you!

Hair	**Body**	**Clothes**
Clean, tidy	Clean shaven (men!)	Clean, ironed
Nothing dramatic	Clean fingernails	Shoes polished, heeled
Out of your eyes	Not too much aftershave or perfume	No drooping hemlines
Don't keep pushing it back	Fresh breath	Flies and zips done up
	No body odour	No dangling buttons
	Keep ear-rings to ears – not in eg noses	Tuck your shirt/ blouse in
		Not too much jewellery

Voice	**Basic manners**	**Attitude**
Speak clearly	Don't swear	Be positive
Don't grunt	Don't smoke	Smile
Don't mumble	Don't chew gum	Thank people who help
Vary the pitch and speed of your voice	Don't pick your nose	Look alert
Don't speak too fast	Be prompt	Don't fiddle
	Don't gaze out of the window	Walk confidently
	Be polite	Shake hands firmly

Fig. 12. Portraying the right image.

Showing the Right Attitude and Image

SUMMARY

- To survive and prosper, being good just isn't good enough. You have to excel.
- Positive Attitude Creates Excellence.
- Be alert, energetic and willing.
- Think about the image you want to create.
- Advertised posts mean lots of competition – why not find another route in?
- Keep copies of everything you send out – including letters asking for information, CVs, application forms *etc.*

CASE STUDIES

Sarah takes positive action

Sarah asked her parents to send her copies of the recruitment pages from local papers weekly so that she could get an idea of what was available. Sarah's parents were so relieved that she was starting to think about her future at last that they agreed. Sarah was surprised to find herself feeling calmer about the future than she had done before. 'It's because you're finally doing something about it,' her father told her.

Matthew smoothes over a problem

Matthew went for a meeting with his tutor to discuss his dissertation. He had hit several problems and needed help. In their discussion, his tutor mentioned that the university was enlisting the help of a local PR company. Matthew took action: he asked his tutor for any names he could give him. Matthew went home, put a letter and CV together and asked for an initial discussion to talk about careers in PR.

Mary continues her search

Another job appeared in the local press, which was not working with young people but would enable Mary to work with young mothers – usually teenagers. This time, the hours did fit. Mary rang up and asked to have an informal meeting with the manager. He was impressed with Mary's enthusiasm, energy and passion for helping people and the fact that Mary had bothered to ring up to ask for an informal interview.

DISCUSSION POINTS

1. As a customer, when was the last time you received service which really made you sit up and take notice? What impact did it have on

your impression of the organisation?

2. What makes a successful organisation? Define success. Who contributes to that success?

3. What would you expect in terms of service from a company that claims to have professional staff? How is this going to affect the staff that work for that organisation?

6
Looking for Work

SOME FIRST THOUGHTS

The good news
- The avenues available for finding work are expanding.
- Many jobs are not filled through advertising but by other routes.
- The more pro-active and creative you are, the more likely you are to find the right job.

Check those deadlines
Firms recruit differently:

- finance and engineering tends to be in the autumn of each year
- the media in March/April
- throughout the year as they need new recruits (especially small and medium sized companies).

Don't ignore non-degree vacancies
If you see a job that appeals but does not specify a degree as an entry requirement, don't automatically pass it over. Many companies don't specify a degree standard of education and the job could prove to be an exciting opportunity to get your foot in the door.

Be sure of your networks
There are two sorts of networks you can use for job hunting:

- people you know form a huge network of contacts – they may be able to put you in touch with people who might take you on
- access to a network of knowledge such as IT, the press.

NETWORKING

Networking with people
Networking involves using a network of contacts you have who may be able to help you get a job.

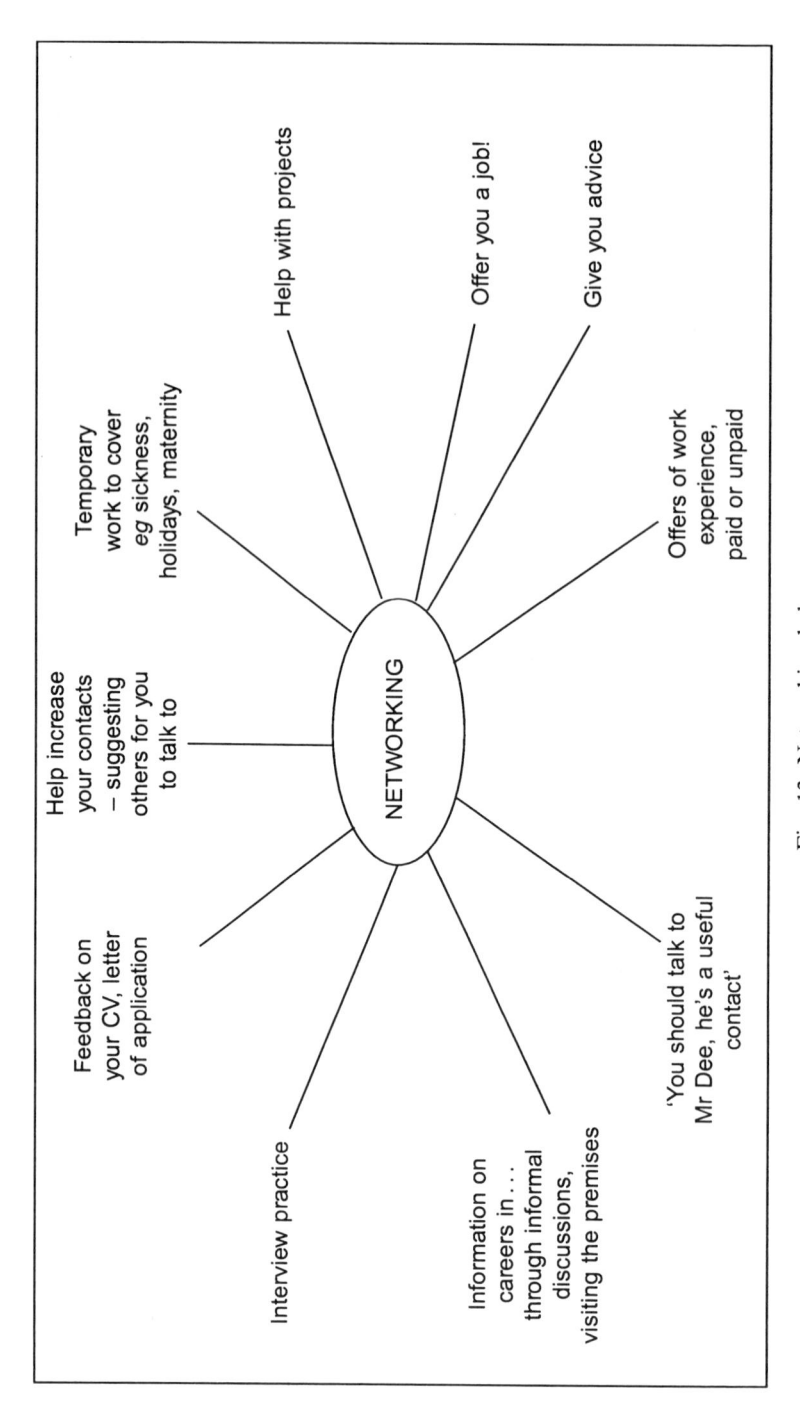

Fig. 13. Networking helps.

Question and answer
I've heard a lot about networking. How can it help me?
Many positions are filled through networking, but it can also offer you other things. For example, most of your contacts will know personnel officers who may be able to give you advice on your CV or interview technique. Alternatively, they may know of someone who is in the field you're interested in.

Do
- be polite – make sure your contact has time to talk to you
- ask if they can suggest other people you should talk to
- write to thank them for their time
- be honest
- know what you can offer a prospective employer before going to see them
- do some homework on the company before you go – it shows genuine interest
- be positive.

Employers are busy people: your networking efforts could solve a recruitment problem for them.

Don't
- be demanding and adopt a 'Give us a job' approach
- talk negatively about suggestions other people in your network have made
- be afraid to approach people you don't know
- be arrogant and assume a 'the world owes me a living' approach.

Establishing your network
You will be surprised at the number of people you know who may be able to help you. List those you know who work.

Immediate family: _____

Relatives: _____

Family friends: _____

School friends: _____

University friends: _____

School staff _____

University staff _____

List employers you know (include name of your contact, size of organisation, what the company does, who you know there):

Work experience at school or
college of further education: _____

Paid holiday/Saturday work: _____

Any full-time posts: _____

Work experience placements
during university course: _____

List people involved in careers advice:

Careers service at home: _____

Careers service at university: _____

Careers staff at school: _____

Professional bodies: _____

Jobcentre – location: _____

TEC: _____

Now:
think of the number of people they could connect you
with via their network.

TECs
Many TECs are starting to concentrate on graduates in their own right, establishing training programmes for them, finding suitable placements and trying to ensure that local employers' needs are met where recruitment purposes are concerned. Do not underestimate the ability of your local TEC to help you: they should have an excellent local knowledge of employers and should also be able to put you in touch with other TECs in the country.

Networking via information

You'll need a network of information-based material as well as your contacts.

Internet/e-mail
Internet is increasingly used as a recruitment tool by many companies, especially in the IT industry. Job hunters can surf the Internet looking for vacancies and even have access to company brochures. *GET* can also be accessed on the Internet at http://www. get.co.uk

JobSite UK (Worldwide) Ltd
JobSite UK (Worldwide) Ltd is an Internet recruitment forum for all employment sectors. Every month, over 400 recruitment consultancies register their vacancies directly onto the JobSite platform, covering all employment sectors. You can access the vacancies on the WWW at http://www.jobsite@jobsite.co.uk or, if you don't have Internet access, send an e-mail to jobsite@jobsite.co.uk specifying the work you want, and preferred location and salary. By visiting the WWW site, job seekers can identify the most suitable vacancies. You can also receive the most suitable jobs by e-mail each day.

JobSite offers access to jobs in specialised fields, including sales and marketing, accounting, engineering, finance, IT, IT sales, secretarial work and lots more. JobSite has a CV distribution service: via the WWW or by e-mail, you can submit an updated CV to all relevant JobSite registered agencies.

PeopleBank the Employment Network
This offers employers a fast and cost-effective way to recruit staff, enabling them to access a database of candidates on their PCs via the Internet.

PeopleBank the Employment Network have a registration form specifically for graduates, in which you specify the work you want, preferred location and salary. You also give details about your skills, qualifications and work experience, along with a brief summary to market your capabilities. This summary is vital as an employer's decision to look at your CV in detail is based on this section.

The process is as follows:

- you send your form to PeopleBank the Employment Network, who register you, or you can register on the Internet

- as employers seek recruits, they enter their selection criteria and a short list of appropriate candidates appears

- employers select those CVs they wish to read from the brief summaries candidates have written
- from these, employers ask PeopleBank the Employment Network to contact those they want to interview
- if this includes you, PeopleBank the Employment Network call you to see if you are interested in the job and organisation; if you are, they release your name and personal details to the employer – you are anonymous until then
- the employer contacts you for an interview at which point PeopleBank the Employment Network withdraw from the process.

The benefits of using this route include:

- PeopleBank the Employment Network saves employers time and money, so more of them are using it
- it gives you a speedy way to market yourself – it saves you time
- you can update your details from anywhere in the world – ideal if you are travelling
- you have access to vacancies employers want to advertise
- it can lead to short-term work – many employers use PeopleBank the Employment Network if they need staff in a hurry.

PCs
These can be helpful in giving you information about CV writing, word processing and so forth. Self-directed tuition is frequently available in local libraries so that you can teach yourself, *eg* Word for Windows or job hunting skills.

Television
Don't forget TV programmes and teletext. There have been useful series about selecting staff and why employers appoint one individual over another.

Libraries
Don't underestimate libraries – *eg* local, university, business libraries – for they have lots of useful information, especially if you want to find out what employers exist in your preferred location and area of work. You will find:

- trade magazines
- national newspapers
- phone directories from towns all over the UK
- information on the European Union
- trade directories such as *Kompass*.

Career booklets
- Vacancy bulletins, *eg Job Opportunities Bulletin, Prospects Today, Prospects for the Finalist*.
- *Hobsons Casebooks*, which provide lots of useful information and case studies relating to specific careers, circumstances and international locations – check your university careers service.
- Specialist journals and publications, available in your university careers service or local libraries.
- Vacancy lists produced by professional bodies: call the appropriate professional body to see if they do this and also careers services. Some of these identify vacancies for the summer or in the immediate future.
- *Graduate Employment & Training (GET)* which lists thousands of graduate jobs, plus information on the companies seeking to recruit, likely training and salaries.

CSU Ltd produces many publications about opportunities for graduates, including booklets on job hunting. These should also be available in your careers service's library. Some careers services produce regional publications and books such as *Graduate Employment and Training (GET)*, are produced annually. For more information, see Further Reading.

Newspapers
Don't restrict yourself to national papers – use local papers too. Your network of friends and family can help, looking for any vacancies or keeping an eye out to see if any firms you may be interested in working for are in the news, *eg* 'Engineering firm wins large contract from French company' may signal an opportunity to send that company your CV and offer your services.

Newspapers provide:

- An idea of the jobs available and the criteria employers are looking for – and addresses to write to for information. Some national

papers dedicate certain days of the week to specific careers.
- Career pages with news of *eg* employment trends *etc*.
- Financial details about the companies you are applying to.
- Updates on company developments, *eg* if a firm is downsizing it may not be a good idea to apply. If you note that a firm is expanding, they may need extra staff, so you could send them a copy of your CV.
- Updates on employment opportunities, technological changes, alterations to professional qualifications *etc*. Read them – they add to your evidence of interest and will enable you to enter a lively discussion with prospective employers.
- Updates on developments that may affect organisations you are applying to. For example, you could be asked in interview: 'What sorts of services do our major competitors offer young people? How can we get ahead of them?'

Networking via professional bodies
These are established to ensure high standards of service and behaviour, protecting the public from cowboy operators, to keep members up to date with developments and changes and to establish programmes of professional training. They usually can help in the following ways:

- lists of members
- lists of members with vacancies to fill
- careers brochures
- training details
- acknowledging that you're a professional
- suggesting skills you need to enter their profession.

WRITING TO EMPLOYERS

Finding them
- *Yellow Pages*, phone book
- trade directories
- local newspapers – who is advertising goods and services
- local news
- local TECs
- your contacts.

Writing on spec
You could write directly to employers to see if they have vacancies available. This shows interest, initiative and seriousness – all qualities employers like.

Start by asking for help
- careers literature (small companies are less likely to have this)
- a period of work experience/work shadowing
- answers to questions you may have
- annual report, accounts, brochure outlining goods and services for public issue
- advice.

Be relevant, don't hassle them and thank them for any help they give you.

Send a CV
Once you've learnt more about the company and you think it matches your needs (*eg* small team, does a lot of project work, looking to expand, good location, like the products), send a covering letter with a CV (see Figure 14). Emphasise your skills and any relevant experience. Explain how their company caught your attention, *eg* 'I was interested to see in the *Daily Echo* that you are expanding your IT section...' and show you've done some research since. 'I see from your annual report that you are planning a new service to customers....' Ask if you could meet to discuss career opportunities within their company.

Remember: people at work are very busy
If a company knows of someone with the personal qualities, attitude and skills that they require, they may recruit directly without advertising – it's quicker and cheaper. This is particularly the case with small companies where delays in finding new recruits can cause much disruption to a business. In larger organisations, personnel staff often dread advertising for fear of the huge number of replies they will receive.

You're also very busy
You may dread the thought of turning up to assessment centres and doing a two-day stint with people you don't know, having managed to battle your way through an application process while CVs and application forms argue for your attention and time when you know you should be finishing your project, writing that essay *etc*. Researching small and medium sized companies can be a very useful way to find a job that provides considerable interest, satisfaction and a real team ethic.

```
                                        121 Hopeful St
                                        St George
                                        (Tel: 0184-98765)


13 March 199X

Mr Jones
Managing Director
Video Systems Ltd
21 Grange Road
St George

Dear Mr Jones,

I was interested to read in the *Weekly News* that your firm is
planning to expand owing to increased business and I wondered
whether you would be interested in the skills and experience I have
to offer?

I am due to graduate with a degree in Media Studies. The course
has been a practical one and has involved work experience with a
variety of companies, thereby giving me the opportunity to use the
skills I have learnt on the course. These include video production,
sound engineering and project management.

I like to work as part of a small team where I can make a real
contribution, so the size of your company appeals. Looking through
your catalogue, I see that you have produced videos on a wide range
of subjects, many of which cover my interests. I feel sure that I could
be of use to your company in developing this side of the business.

I would very much like to meet you to discuss the opportunities
available within your company in this competitive market. If I may, I
will call you at the beginning of next week to arrange a time to meet.

Yours sincerely



Ben Cooke
```

Fig. 14. Writing on spec.

Think broadly

If you get an interview but there are no opportunities available within the company at that time, ask if they can suggest other people you might talk to and then keep in touch. Follow up the initial discussion with a letter to thank them for their time; reiterate your interest in the firm; explain how you can be contacted in the future.

Other routes in

When you are starting this search, you could offer your services on a temporary basis. A time-waster for companies can be getting temporary staff in, especially if they are different people every time. Organisations need cover for:

- maternity leave
- holidays
- times of the year when the workload is particularly heavy
- lengthy absence due to illness
- staff who have left and not been replaced.

You could offer to cover for these. The company benefits because they will have a 'temp' who is familiar with it, so they don't have to start explaining everything each time you go back. If they like you, you could end up with a full-time job. At the least, you could get paid work experience and a good reference.

SIGNING UP WITH RECRUITMENT AGENCIES

Recruitment agencies can make job hunting easier, but you must be prepared to talk about your skills, career interests, values and needs and explain what you want to do. Don't expect the agency to offer careers advice and do all your career thinking for you.

Using an agency has pros and cons

Likely pros
- a good knowledge of local employment opportunities
- advice on your CV
- already have employers looking for recruits
- free service to you
- offer a temping service
- offer an exciting career themselves, especially if you like selling
- may be nationwide, so could help you find work elsewhere in Britain.

Likely cons
- cowboy agencies exist
- don't sit at home and wait for them to call you – keep in touch
- doesn't necessarily guarantee you a job
- may try to encourage you to take something you don't really want.

Specialist areas
- some professional bodies have their own recruitment agency
- graduates sections
- overseas divisions
- language specialists
- specialists in a career area, *eg* law, banking, media sales.

Checking the agency out
Good agencies:

- tend to be national – they share nationwide vacancies
- talk to you about your skills and strengths
- test your competencies in appropriate areas
- are members of FRES (their professional body) with qualified staff
- set out what they can and cannot do for you in a brochure or contract
- visit employers before they send candidates
- brief you prior to interviews and de-brief you afterwards.

Avoid others which:

- try to push you into work which is clearly unsuitable
- don't tell you anything about the employer you are going to visit.

Susan signs up for temporary work
'I signed up with an agency to temp. My consultant was never on time for my appointments and he tried to persuade me to go to an office to use a system which I hadn't used before. I left and went to an organisation I'd seen advertised in *The Times*. They were far more professional: they even tested my spelling!'

Making contact
Make an appointment to meet a consultant. Take your CV and dress appropriately – image is important, as the agency has to recommend you to their clients. A consultant will talk to you about your skills, qualifications, experience and career aspirations and the local employment market. Many people sign up with several agencies,

particularly if they want to get some temporary work while looking for a permanent post. The agency will call you if something comes in but keep in touch on a weekly basis regardless.

ATTENDING ORGANISED EVENTS

Careers conventions

These may be run nationally (*eg* London's Graduate Fair) or locally at various times of the year. Employers attend to promote themselves to would-be recruits or to start the recruitment process; professional bodies use the opportunity to represent their members on a national basis. These events are generally organised by university careers services. Identify what you want to get out of an event before you go and it will be far more valuable. Conventions can provide a useful introduction to prospective organisations which recruit graduates, either in terms of marketing yourself as a possible recruit or finding more information on careers as a graduate. Your careers service will be able to give you details of forthcoming events.

Do some groundwork
Find out which employers will be there before you go and get any information you can on them, *eg* the services they offer, career brochures *etc*. When you approach their representatives, you can then show that you have done some initial research and are more likely to have good questions to ask. Do dress appropriately and take your CV along, making it relevant to your preferred career choice.

Once you're there
Stands may be extremely busy, so you may not get much of an opportunity to make an impression. Be ready to:

- give a brief overview of your skills and relevant work experience
- show you've done some research – have some questions to ask.

You could always follow up by writing to an employer saying 'Thank you for your time at the Careers Exhibition recently' and ask pertinent questions which show you've given further thought to your conversation.

Make use of any sessions run alongside the fair, *eg* on writing a CV (can you improve on yours?) or 'where to start'.

Presentations

Employers may give a presentation about their firm, their career opportunities and what they look for in prospective recruits at the university campus or at a nearby hotel. Most employers are very helpful and will expand a little to talk about opportunities generally, although they are obviously looking to recruit to their own organisation. They want to meet you, so take advantage of their coming to campus. If an employer is looking to recruit people with specialist knowledge (*eg* engineers) he may head straight for the appropriate student society on campus.

The milkround
Your careers service will distribute information on those employers who will be visiting your university specifically to interview students for vacancies: the 'milkround'. Fewer employers are attending the milkround as they find it is not so cost-effective in terms of time and money. Closing dates to apply for an interview vary so make a point of visiting your careers service at the very start of the autumn term. The employers draw up a short list of students they wish to see and the service draws up an interview timetable. Don't forget to research the employer and competition thoroughly!

Your department
Your department may have strong links with various employers, particularly if it is involved in research or training. Find out if staff there have any contacts they could point you towards.

WORKING FOR YOURSELF

You could create your own job, either by suggesting to a company that they might be able to use your skills on a contract basis or by setting up on your own and running your own business. Many people seek the satisfaction of working for themselves and not somebody else but there are pros and cons.

Pros
- satisfaction of running your own business
- can work at home and save the hassle and cost of travelling
- control in developing the business as you see fit
- not hampered by company bureaucracy
- may fit in more readily with family commitments
- self-reliance – you could have been made redundant anyway by a firm
- flexible lifestyle.

Cons
- finding the money to set up
- could run into financial problems
- can be more stressful working away from an office and a social environment
- must be disciplined
- work can easily overspill into life at home
- no one around to bounce ideas off
- you run the entire show – no time to be sick: You *are* The Firm!

Contracting
Contracting is also an option if you've got specific skills to offer. The work to be undertaken, deadlines and price are negotiated and agreed between you and the company.

Franchising
The main advantage of getting involved in a franchise is that the product has already been tried out and tested. You will probably find that the franchiser will give you training and start-up help. It can be an expensive business to get into, however.

There are plenty of opportunities for people who can market themselves and their skills, who have a head for business and who have an original idea. Research is vital, so that you can check out what the competition is offering and move ahead.

FINDING WORK ABROAD

Some ways of looking for work abroad are listed below.

Tick when you have:

Talked to locals about how to get work in that country	_____
Used the Internet	_____
Read local/national papers and magazines	_____
Talked to local employers and recruitment agencies	_____
Contacted the local Chamber of Commerce to see if they can help	_____
Had a good look through the information available at your university careers service	_____

Checked what programmes or contacts your
department or other departments have which
could be useful to you   ____

Talked to employers connected with your
university about contacts they may have, either
through work or through their own activities
outside work (*eg* international service clubs such
as Rotary, Lions Clubs)   ____

Talked to foreign students on campus to find
out how locals get jobs back home   ____

Contacted the country's embassy for advice on visas *etc* ____

Looked into obtaining a work placement as part of
your degree or in addition to it (*eg* through AIESEC)
(or IAESTE for engineers)   ____

Spent summer holidays abroad to make local contacts   ____

Contacted British firms with departments abroad
to find out 'What's the best way in?'   ____

Looked into programmes sponsored by the EU
which may help   ____

Found out how to write a CV that is appropriate
for the country you want to work in   ____

Points to consider
- How can you show an employer you could adapt to working abroad?

- Can you display language competencies? How can you improve your language skills?

- Have you got relevant work experience to offer or experience that provides evidence of your skills base?

MORE TIPS ON GETTING A JOB

When you are deciding which employers to apply to for work, you should think about these points:

- What are the organisation's goals? How could you contribute to its direction?

- What products and/or services does it sell and do these excite you?

- Is there anything happening locally, nationally or internationally which could affect it, *eg* a change of government, crash in the stock market, take-over by a competitor?
- What does the job involve?
- Who are its major competitors? Might you want to apply to them as well/ instead?
- Is the company expanding?
- What could the firm do for you (training, gaining experience, building on skills, promotion opportunities)?
- What can you do for it?
- Where are the immediate vacancies? Would you have to move?

And some more advice
- Keep a pen that works and clean paper to write on by the telephone – people always ring when you least expect them to!

Creating opportunities
- Turn negative responses into **positive leads**, *eg* 'I know you're not recruiting, but can you suggest someone else I should talk to?'
- You could ask the personnel officer if there will be any vacancies in the future or if there are any other vacancies which might interest you in the firm.

CASE STUDIES

Sarah signs up with recruitment agencies
At home for the Christmas holidays, Sarah went in to sign up with local recruitment agencies to find out what they could offer her. 'What can *you* offer *us*?' they replied. Sarah described the IT aspects of her course and her market research experience. 'Come back and see us next time you're home,' they said. Sarah did and she spent two weeks in a bank at Easter and got lots of contacts through the social life that went with it.

Matthew's work experience helps him
Matthew decided PR was for him. His week with a local firm had helped and he'd spoken to two or three friends in that line of work. Matthew wrote directly to companies, most of which advised, 'Get

some work experience'. Michael always called them up to ask if he could have some with their company. By the end of the Easter term, he had a couple of places lined up ready for the summer.

Mary prepares to apply

Mary had a useful discussion with the manager, who explained that they would be recruiting two advisers and one trainee. Mary decided to apply, but she also wanted a plan B, so she kept looking in the local papers and visiting the local library for current vacancies. She also got her references into gear – her course tutor and a local priest volunteered – and did what research she could to update herself on what other authorities in the country were doing on helping young mothers. She wanted to put her application forward with some ideas.

DISCUSSION POINTS

1. If you were recruiting for your organisation, how much research would you expect applicants to have done to show they were genuinely interested in a job?

2. What are the advantages and disadvantages of applying to vacancies advertised in the press?

3. What can you learn from other people's experiences of applying for jobs?

7
Marketing Yourself

GETTING READY

Whatever method you use to find a job, you should find yourself with a shortlist of companies which appeal to you. Compare them in terms of what they offer and how they fit in with **you** and your likes, values and needs. Which one gives you the most buzz?

If you are to be successful in getting a job, you need to know:

- what you can offer
- who prospective employers are and what they look for in a prospective recruit
- who is in charge of recruitment
- what the next step is.

Then:

- make contact
- be ready to attend interviews/informal chats, *ie* plan for possible disruption to studies, prepare your image, study interview technique, practise psychometric tests.

Are you right for the job?

1. What does the work involve? (Talk to people who do similar work, get a job description, check the literature on this career in the careers service – can they put you in touch with past graduates doing similar work?)

2. What skills and personal qualities are required to do the work? Can you provide evidence that you have them?

3. Does it meet your values and needs, *eg* location, size of firm *etc*?

4. Look back through the skills and strengths you identified earlier – have you really got them?

5. Find out as much as you can about the company.

If you like the answers, then go for it!

MAKING CONTACT

If you are responding to an advert, employers may:

- request a CV (you'll need to do a covering letter too)
- ask you to write or call for further information.

When you write to the advertiser to ask for more information make sure you mention the vacancy and the publication you saw it in by name.

When you have done your research and the further information arrives from the company – if there is any – you will be in a better position to ascertain whether you should apply. Probe more deeply:

Have you got what they want?
- Skills, abilities, qualifications?
- Other requirements, *eg* languages, driving licence, knowledge of IT systems?
- Other preferable qualities, *eg* well informed on current affairs, public speaking skills, interest in social issues, knowledge of financial markets *etc?*
- Can you satisfactorily cover for things they want that you don't have, *eg* provide a strategy to cover weaknesses in your application?

'One year's work experience please'
You don't have to have one solid year. You could gather that year's experience through summer holiday jobs, part-time employment in the term, voluntary work *etc.*

Highlighting yourself

Concentrate on what you can do for them
Jean recruits students every year for a training scheme. 'Applicants always describe what the scheme can do for them, but not what they can do for the scheme,' she says. 'When I do get someone who explains what *they* can contribute, it's like a breath of fresh air. I want to see them immediately.' So talk about the skills and qualities you can offer them.

'I want this position because...'
Employers want to know that you really want to work for them and that you really, really, really want the job! So show employers why they appeal in particular. Explain how your research has led you to believe that they are the right firm for you – and you for them – and the reasons why the position appeals.

Make the link between work and your degree
Don't expect employers to know all about qualifications because many employers are totally confused by them. Explain what your course has covered.

Clear up any doubts about your course
Many employers don't know if courses are academic or vocational any more, especially in subjects such as 'Media studies' which could involve a considerable degree of practical work or a large amount of academic research. It is therefore much more important to put lots of information on your CV, outlining what your course has covered and emphasising how much it relates to the workplace.

If your course is clearly an academic one, *eg* English Literature, you will need to place emphasis on skills and qualities you have developed over the course unless your subject is directly relevant to the job you are applying for.

WRITING YOUR COVERING LETTER AND CV

The covering letter
- The covering letter is crucial.
- Take time to write it.
- It should encourage the employer to read your CV.

See Figure 15 for an example.

Your CV
The aim of writing a CV is to get an interview, so relevance and a professional production are the keys to success:

To the bin	*To an interview*
Scruffy copy with stains	Crisp, clean, original copy
CVs with spelling errors	No spelling mistakes
Double-sided paper	One side of A4 only
Too many pages	Keep to two sheets if possible
Lots of irrelevant waffle	Be relevant – leave everything else out

Little Grove House
Blackheath
London RRR RRR
(Tel: 0181-111-111)

Mrs L Pearson
Personnel Manager
Risky Banking Ltd
1 Fallaway Street
London SSS SSS

25 September 199X

Dear Mrs Pearson

Graduate Trainee

Further to your advertisement in the *Evening Standard*, I write to apply for the above post.

I am in my final year at the University of Zest and am seeking to gain an entry position into the finance sector. I spent a summer working with Barclays Bank which gave me an excellent insight into the banking world and enabled me to develop my knowledge and understanding of financial institutions, especially as I spent time finding out what products other banks offer young people. In order to increase my awareness of the finance sector, I arranged to spend a week with an investment bank, which certainly highlighted the exciting careers finance has to offer.

My experience at university thus far has afforded me the opportunity to develop interpersonal skills through my academic studies and extra-curricular responsibilities; to enhance my abilities to work in a team, to present report findings to a variety of audiences and to make contact with a variety of people within the finance sector.

I was interested to read in the *Financial Times* that your bank will be extending its services to British nationals working in the European Union and marketing them accordingly. I also understand from reading your company literature that you have plans to extend your role in Eastern Europe. I am looking for a firm to which I can contribute my energy, enthusiasm and teamwork while receiving training and support for career development in return. I particularly enjoy working on projects and am very driven to achieve targets and goals I set myself.

I enclose my CV for your information and would be happy to attend for an interview at any time.

Yours sincerely

Frank Jones

Fig. 15. Writing a covering letter.

Lots of jargon	Expand on abbreviations, no jargon
Addressed to no one in particular	Find out who is in charge of application
Flippancy, attempts to be humorous	Show seriousness
Inconsistent layout	Make the layout consistent throughout
Hand-written	Word-processed

What should a CV include?
- full name
- address and phone number – both term-time (put dates) and home
- nationality
- date of birth
- secondary and tertiary education to date
- work history
- interests and hobbies
- names of two referees
- any personal details which could add weight to your application, *eg* 'clean full driving licence'
- any evidence of achievements, *eg* 'Won prize for conversational French in the sixth form' if you are applying for a job where languages are useful.

Questions and answers
I'm a mature student. Should I put my date of birth on the CV or will it put employers off?
Put everything else first to excite the employer and make him think 'yes, this person looks good'. If you leave your age off, it may make the reader suspicious. Add it at the end as your date of birth, rather than your age.

How much weight should I give to each of my stages in education?
The most weight should go to the most recent part of your education, *ie* your degree (or post-graduate degree). This is particularly important as employers become increasingly confused by the sheer range of courses available which could either have vocational or academic leanings. Give the results of your A-Levels or GNVQ course (explain what GNVQ stands for and what it covered). Keep your GCSE results to a minimum and stress those which the employer is likely to be most interested in, *eg* 'Ten GCSEs, including Mathematics (B), English Language (C) and French (A). All other subjects over C grade'. Ignore primary education altogether.

Should I put my education and work experience etc in the order I did them? Or the most recent first?
Put the most recent things you've done first in each category. Employers want to know where you are at *now* because *now* is going to lead on into employment.

Different types of CV
A range of CVs is available and you need to decide what is most appropriate for the organisation you want to apply for and the position you want. If the employer is looking for high academic achievement, you will need to stress yours and also add any prizes or awards you have gained for outstanding work.

Specialist knowledge
If you are applying for a job where specialist knowledge is required, such as engineering, law, medicine, architecture *etc*, it is particularly vital to show:

- what your course has covered in terms of your subject – list each unit or course subject and the grade you obtained in it (so that the employer can see where your strengths and weaknesses are)
- any exemptions you have gained as a result of your degree
- any societies you belong to that are relevant to your degree or future job, *eg* either university societies or professional bodies
- any add-on skills you have developed such as business awareness, computer literacy, foreign languages, willingness to re-locate, clean driving licence, project work
- evidence of relevant work experience
- proof that your level of interest extends to beyond work, *eg* subscriber to trade magazines, working on designing cars as a hobby
- evidence of research into the career itself, *eg* taking advantage of any talks, open days, visits to engineering work.

Show your passion for the work.

Skills-based CV
This is useful where you've done lots of different jobs and need to gloss over the fact that you've moved from one to another.

Communicator: I spent a year working in a variety of businesses in Manchester. This improved my communication skills, as I worked with a variety of people at all different levels; it also taught me to think on my feet. My course has increased my confidence further, as it has involved giving presentations to small groups and a large audience.

Promoter: I particularly enjoyed promoting the concert our Student Union organised in aid of 'Save the Children'. Our target audience was 2,000; we sold 2,400 tickets, not just within the university but also outside it. My promotion campaign involved speaking on local radio, designing leaflets to put up around the city and writing an article for the *Manchester Gazette*.

Chronological CV
The standard CV, as produced in Figure 16. Frank Jones is applying for a job in a bank. You will need to find a way of writing a CV that you feel comfortable with: Frank has chosen to highlight in bold those areas which he thinks are particularly relevant to banking.

Referees
- Are your referees willing to provide a reference for you?
- Do they know what you are applying for?
- Have they got a copy of your CV and any relevant details of the job, *eg* copy of the advertisement, job description, *etc* so that they can fully comment on your suitability for the position?
- Let them know the result.

COMPLETING THE APPLICATION FORM

Application forms come in all guises. Some employers use their own, while others prefer applicants to complete the standard application form, obtainable from the careers service. Whichever form you complete, you can increase your chances of getting to the interview stage.
Don't reduce your chances through:

1. Illegible handwriting.
2. Spelling errors.
3. Ignoring instructions.

Frank Jones

Home address
Flat 3, Hiddlecrick Road
Greenedge
Leicester
(Tel: 01532-342424)
(Dates: 21.3.97 21.4.97)

Term-time address
Smedly Cottage
Lala Avenue
Zest
(Tel: 01111-22345)
(Dates: 21.4.97 – 01.7.97)

Educational history

1994-97 **BA (Hons) in Business Studies at the University of Zest (2:1 expected)**

My studies covered:

Marketing	Financial Accounting
Banking Procedures	Human Resource Management
Change Management	Information Technology
Total Quality Management	Economics
Statistics	Psychology

- Subjects were assessed by means of examinations, projects and assignments.
- Frequently, our projects were set by employers who had genuine problems for teams of us to solve.

My final year project was:
Identifying banking requirements for local elderly residents.

- I developed skills in devising questionnaires, research, data analysis, interviewing technique, identifying opportunities for business development in the market, and oral and written presentation skills.
- I succeeded in my goal to identify the requirements of the elderly: three out of my four recommendations are being discussed further.

1992-1994 **A Levels** in Economics (A), English (C) and Maths (B) (Greenedge Comprehensive School)

1990-1992 **8 GCSEs** including English Language (C), Mathematics (A) and French (B). All other GCSEs exceeded a C grade. (Greenedge Comprehensive School)

Employment History

Summer 1996 **Assistant at Barclays Bank**, Greenedge
- gained an insight into banking, as I spent time in different departments covering for people on holiday; this increased my ability to cope with change and my interest in banking as a career. I was impressed by the way everyone worked together to achieve the bank's objectives.

Fig. 16. Writing a CV.

Summer 1994 – 1995	**Sales Assistant**, Gregory's Wine and Cheese Store, The Mall, Greenedge. This developed my skills in: – planning (I ordered new stock every week) – working as a team with manager and four other part-time staff – working under pressure – business awareness, including customer care, working with people.
Summer 1993	Spent the summer undertaking a variety of **temporary roles** for Lockdown Agency, which increased my confidence and increased my ability to cope with change. These roles included: – four weeks computer inputting in an **investment bank** – two weeks as a messenger for a pharmaceutical company The investment bank kindly offered me a week's work shadowing, an experience which I welcomed. The week persuaded me investment banking was not for me.

Skills and interests

Sailing:	**President of the Sailing Club** at University; – enjoyed leading a committee of eight to plan the year's activities – organised three sailing competitions with other universities – planned and enjoyed a week's sailing holiday for 30 British students in Greece.
Hockey:	**Treasurer of the Hockey Club** at University. – budgeted for five trips away in final year – determination enabled us to raise enough money for extra trips away – administered bank account – all records kept up to date and gave me good insight into the role of Treasurer; worked closely with President – committed to training three times a week.

Other points of interest:
- **regular reader** of the *Financial Times*, *Wall Street Journal* and books written by management gurus, including John Harvey-Jones and Tom Peters
- working knowledge of **computer systems**, including Word for Windows, Powerpoint and Excel
- **conversational French**
- clean driving licence
- date of birth: 9 June 1976
- willing to relocate in or out of Britain.

Referees:

Professor Fred Enger Marketing Tutor University of Zest Zest ZT1 XYZ	Mr F. Logan The Manager Littlehampton Bank Peach Tree Avenue Newtown NE2 3TH

4. Filling in the wrong form, *eg* you've completed a standard application form when the company wanted you to complete one of their own.
5. Attaching extra pieces of paper, *eg* your CV, to the form when it distinctly says that they are not to be included.
6. Failing to include job title/reference number if it is requested.

Increasing your chances
1. Read the form through. Photocopy it first and practise completing it.
2. Answer all the questions carefully and relevantly – think about what the selectors want.
3. Take time over it.
4. Answer the questions – don't just put 'see attached CV'.
6. Get the name and title of the right person to send it to.
7. Use the 'Additional Information' section to highlight anything of relevance to the application which will strengthen your chances of success.

Question and answer
Why is it so important to complete the application form properly? It's a pain filling them all out – surely the company can get what they want from my CV and application letter? And do I have to complete every section?

A common reason people are not successful in job applications is that they don't complete the form properly. Employers want you to complete it because it immediately gives them a way to compare you with all the other applicants. Failing to complete it properly indicates that you can't be bothered to make the effort – not a good beginning.

What would your answers be to the questions below?

1. Describe a problem you have faced. How did you approach it? What difficulties did you encounter and how was the problem solved? How differently would you deal with it if faced with a similar problem again?
2. Describe a project you completed as a team. What was the background to the project? What role did you play? Did the team fulfil its goal? Could you have achieved it differently?
3. What appeals to you about our company? And this position?
4. Describe an event you organised. What was the scope of it? What

problems did you encounter and how did you determine whether or not it was successful?

5. Where do you expect to be in ten years' time?
6. What can you contribute to our organisation?
7. Describe an event you were in charge of organising. What was your approach and how did you encourage your team to achieve the desired results?

Back up any mention of interest in the firm or job with evidence. Refer to your list of achievements and experience – it will make the process easier. Application forms are designed to see if you can evaluate your efforts and achievements: so they may ask you to explain the background, describe the action you took and give the result.

Prepare strategies to cover weaknesses
- Yes, I failed my GCSE maths but I re-took it and got a B after tuition at evening classes.
- Yes, I changed jobs a lot in the year before going to university. It helped me to develop a very flexible attitude and to pick things up extremely quickly. I also learned to work with many different people.

Finally
- Copy everything you send.
- Get it checked before sending it.

COPING WITH THE INTERVIEW

The selection process
Some companies use computers to make an initial selection of candidates. Answer all the questions on the application form, even if you are uncertain of the answer, *eg* you aren't sure what grade you might get. Otherwise, the computer will pick up any gaps and may throw your application out!

The selection process can be lengthy or brief, depending on the size of the company, their application process and the amount of work they have on at the moment.

Making contact
The employer responds to your application and you've got an interview. If you are asked to call to make an appointment:

- have your papers in front of you
- know who you need to speak to
- if they are in a meeting, leave a message with details of how to contact you
- be brief – don't waffle
- speak clearly
- ask who will be present at the interview.

Do your homework

Much of your success will lie in your preparation. Expect to be nervous – the interviewers may be as well, because recruiting people is a costly and time-consuming business. Remember that research shows interest, commitment, thoroughness and seriousness – you'll stand out at once.

Research data could include:

- career brochures
- annual report and accounts
- recent achievements of the company, *eg* highlighted in a professional magazine or newspaper
- informal meetings with the employer
- informal visits, arranged by your careers service or you
- visiting showrooms/shops to check out products and services
- checking out what the competition is doing
- reading about events which could affect the company in future.

For example, if you are applying for a position in the financial services industry, you should be able to show that you have an active interest in it and be able to talk about matters relevant to it

- read the *Financial Times* and the business pages of newspapers including those from abroad, *eg* the *Wall Street Journal*
- read recent copies of the *Investors Chronicle, The Economist, Newsweek*
- listen to business programmes on television, eg *The Money Programme*
- find out what the bank's competitors are doing and the sort of services they offer
- be familiar with banking terminology.

Prior to the day
- check your outfit is cleaned and pressed
- get a hair cut
- work out how to get there – allow lots of time for delays (a trial run is often a good idea)
- re-read your notes on the firm, the career, your application
- on the day, prepare your image as outlined in Chapter 5
- check you've got what you need to take.

Almost your turn
- arrive a good ten minutes before you are due
- if very nervous, walk round the block to work off excess energy
- be polite to everyone you meet
- smile!
- check your appearance
- damp hands? wipe them on a hanky or tissue (discreetly in your pocket/handbag)
- cold hands? warm them up – rub them together.

'Come in, please'
- take a deep breath
- walk confidently in
- as you are introduced to people, shake hands firmly, make eye contact and smile
- call people 'Mr Johnson,' 'Miss Way' and not 'Clive' or 'Sarah'
- don't smoke, even if you are offered a cigarette.

The interview
Usually, one staff member has been given charge of the interview; he introduces you to everyone. To kick off, there will probably be some comments about your journey ('You found us all right, then!' or 'Did you find somewhere to park?'), the weather, or even 'How are you?' This is designed to settle you down and help you relax. However awful the journey was or you're feeling, be positive. 'The parking round here is terrible', doesn't get you off to a good start, even if the staff know it to be true.

Roles of the interviewers
Most interviewers will give you an idea of what format the interview will be. Some companies ask all interviewees the same questions to give everyone a fair chance. Others expect the interview to be a two-way conversation. If there is more than one interviewer, each may have a

specific area to cover, *eg*

Personnel manager:	– checking statements you've made on your application – covering the ins and outs of company benefits – checking on any legal requirements.
Prospective boss:	– what appeals to you about the job – the skills you can give him – how you will fit in to the team.

You may find that an extra person takes notes throughout the whole interview, which can be off-putting, but he has been given this specific task and is unlikely to ask you any questions.

In a badly organised interview, everyone talks at once, people ask the same questions or they even start discussing company events and policies amongst themselves.

How will they assess me?
Many interviewers will rank you against set criteria that have been designed for the purpose of selecting candidates, *eg* they may have ten predetermined skills and abilities that they are looking for and rank all the candidates on a 1 to 5 basis, depending on your answers. Smaller companies are less likely to use such criteria. All the interview panel will probably have copies of your application plus they may have to complete evaluation forms on you (often after you have left).

What will they ask?
The questions recruiters ask and the kind of answers they are looking for vary according to the job in hand and the company itself, but the following will probably be included. How would you respond?

- Why do you want to work here?
- How long would you want to work here?
- Where do you want to be five/ten years from now?
- Tell us about a problem you solved.
- What are your strengths?
- Why should we select you rather than anyone else?
- What appeals to you most about this job?
- Give an example of your commitment to a project.
- What do you like to do in your spare time?
- What research have you done into this career?

- Why did you study... and what made you select the University of...?
- Specialist and technical knowledge (if this is relevant to the post).
- How current events may affect the industry, *eg* 'What is your view on...?'
- Surprise questions, *eg* 'What do you feel strongly about?' (designed to see if you can think on your feet).

Many questions will be:

- asked to put you under pressure to see how you react
- connected with situations that occur in the organisation to see how practical your approach is to problem-solving
- to establish how much thought you put into your career planning and development.

Use your research
Use your preparation to relate your experiences, strengths, skills and interests to the job you are applying for – and to show the company what you can do for it.

What can I ask them?
Interviewing should be a two-way process: the interviewers are trying to establish whether you will fit into their firm, you are trying to ascertain further whether it's right for you! You could ask:

- about training support
- company direction
- what the interviewer likes about the company
- how many other applicants there are
- how most people join the firm.

Coming to the end

'Have you got any questions?'	If you have, ask them. If you haven't because they've all been covered during the course of the interview, say so.
'Is there anything else we should know?'	This is a hint that you should wrap up with a conclusion about you. Make it clear that you want the job and why, and state the skills and personal abilities you can bring. Find out what happens next.

Your next step
- The interview is over, but you still have to leave! Say goodbye to people as you go – thank them again for any help they've given you.
- Leave the premises; go somewhere you can relax. Have a good stretch and feel all the tension leave you.
- Write to thank the main interviewer. Reiterate any points you want to stress or to pick up on anything you felt was not covered during the interview which would be relevant to them.
- Evaluate your performance. What did you answer well? Could you have covered some points more effectively? Did you establish a rapport with everyone? How did you handle the more stressful parts of the interview? What would you do differently next time? Talk to your careers adviser about it.

Some companies are willing to talk through your performance with you afterwards if you are not chosen to go forward or are not ultimately offered the job. It is always worth getting any feedback you can, but don't become demanding if it is not forthcoming.

COPING WITH THE NEXT ROUND

Recruitment methods differ
Some companies may appoint on the basis of one interview only, whereas others – especially larger firms – may call you forward for another interview. This could be in one of several forms, including:

Second interview days
These will not necessarily last a whole day and in some cases you may simply be called back to meet with an extra one or two members of staff, depending on the size of the firm. You have another opportunity to ask questions, and they can assess further how you may fit into the organisation. Sometimes, this interview is merely a rubber stamp to a decision already taken, but you may also be given the chance to look around the premises and meet more of the staff.

Again, preparation is vital. Probe further this time. You should be given an idea of what the day will be like, who will be there, how many of you will be interviewed on the day, and what the day should consist of. You may find that you are asked similar questions to your first interview but in greater depth.

Larger companies may summon you suddenly to an **assessment**

Marketing Yourself

centre for a couple of days with a group of six to eight other applicants to go through exercises, interviews, tests and presentations. They want to see how you work as a team. Everyone will be a little nervous – but try to control your nerves and relax. You will probably learn a lot from the day – and after all, all the candidates are in the same boat. Support each other! Exercises usually relate closely to the work you would be doing with the company.

Group exercises
These are common where a group of prospective candidates have been called up for a second interview day. You may be given a subject to discuss as a group and observers from the company will watch you as you debate it. They are looking to see how well everyone works as a team and will assess you for your contribution, how you encouraged others, whether you were able to persuade others to see your point of view, if you kept the group to the point and whether you displayed leadership qualities.

In-tray exercise
You may be given information about the company and then a tray of work to prioritise to see how you work under pressure, how you assimilate details and organise your workload.

Written work
You may have a written piece of work to do within a given time frame to see how you react under pressure, whether you can communicate clearly and grasp a subject and the issues involved quickly.

Testing your knowledge
If you are applying for work in commerce or business, some firms may ask you about money markets, business terminology and so forth to find out how much you know and to test your interest.

Personality tests
You may be given a number of questions to answer – there is no right or wrong answer, it depends on your personality and these give the employer a chance to find out what your personality is like. Be honest!

Aptitude tests
Designed to test your verbal, numerical and/or diagrammatic reasoning. Many careers services will have examples of these – try a few so you know what to expect and can practise!

Presentations
Presentations help selectors assess how clearly you can put over a subject. You may be asked to prepare a subject for delivery for the day or you may find that you are asked to speak on a subject off the top of your head, or with a restricted amount of time for preparation. Get something lined up just in case you have to do a five- or ten-minute presentation without warning.

Interviews as part of the day
This could be with one or two people or a panel interview, where you will meet three or four people at once. In an organised interview, more important for a panel interview, the panel should have decided in advance how they wanted to play the interview. One person may be acting as an observer and may not say a word during the whole process – don't be put off by this, or by the fact that they may be taking notes!

Informal lunches/breakfasts
A 'getting to know you and us' exercise, often described as 'informal'. You are still 'on display' so don't drink alcohol or smoke. You may have a good time but will you do yourself any favours with the selectors?

Following up
Write and thank the person who was in charge of the day, stress your interest in joining the firm and reiterate any skills you have.

Friends already at work may have good advice to give you following their recruitment experiences and be able to tell you more about the process from the interviewee end.

REMEMBER

- A professional approach and preparation are key to success.
- Create the right image.
- Expect to be nervous – it is only natural!

CASE STUDIES

Sarah finds a job of interest
Sarah was interested in a job in the local tourism office offering a one-year contract researching all the tourist attractions in her home town and talking to visitors to see what they thought of them. She applied, stressing her experience of market research, her report-writing abilities, and her liking for places of interest – her drama background had taken

her into plenty of places of them. She got an interview – and the job!

Matthew doesn't prepare

Matthew applied for a job as a trainee. He sent his CV off, with a covering letter to the firm, describing his research efforts to date and his work experience placements. At the interview, however, Michael realised his preparation was insufficient: he had discovered who the chairman was, but had little other knowledge of the firm. Nor did he read back over his career management file to remind himself of what he could offer this prospective employer. Consequently he was flustered at interview and didn't get the job.

Mary applies for a post

Mary sent in her form to apply for the post working with young mothers. She stressed her listening skills, her experience with young people, the counselling and practical elements of her course and the projects she had done that were relevant to the post. Mary was invited for interview and had to prepare a ten-minute presentation on the role of social services in assisting young people. She spent the weekend preparing for her interview and working on her presentation. Her homework paid off – she was successful.

DISCUSSION POINTS

1. What would you be looking for in a candidate who was applying for a place on a management training programme?

2. What impression would you like to make in the first three minutes of an interview?

3. 'Tell us about yourself.' What would you include? (Remember, be brief and relevant.)

8
Dealing with Common Obstacles and Barriers

COPING WITH REJECTION

Is it worth trying again?
If you think you gave the application your best shot, don't brood over it but make sure you learn from your experience. Ask for any **feedback** the company can give you on the presentation of your CV, application form and interview technique. Don't press, hassle, argue or become aggressive if they are unable to do so – it could be company policy not to provide feedback.

Handling frequent rejections
Ask yourself:

- Do I need to alter my interview technique?
- Or change my image?
- What exactly goes wrong?
- Am I aiming too high or too low?
- Does my CV need changing?

Seek advice and help from recruiters themselves. Most people in your network will have contacts with those in charge of recruiting. Ask them if they would put you in touch with a personnel officer for a quick discussion about your CV and interview technique.

Six weeks or a few months later
The situation could have changed and a similar position might become available, so if you are really keen on a firm, keep politely reminding them that you are there and keep them in touch with your progress on the job hunting process.

LACKING WORK EXPERIENCE

If you can show interest and commitment in your intended career by undertaking some form of relevant work experience, you'll have an immediate strategic advantage:

- it shows you're motivated
- you'll be more effective at work because you'll have a basic knowledge of business, business culture and technology and so adapt more quickly
- you can prove yourself, *eg* with a reference
- you might find yourself with a job offer – 'Come back and work for us full time after you've graduated' – it gives you and the employer a chance to see how you work together.

So when could I get some?
Try the Christmas/Easter/summer holidays, free days/hours at university, weekends, evenings, whatever. The longer the stint, the more you will get out of it.

How do I get it?
- Use your contacts - 'do you know of anyone in the... industry?'
- Ask the careers service to put you in touch with a firm – they may have details of vacancies and/or placements, *eg* for the summer in or out of the UK.
- Ask your local TEC for help.
- Try temping.
- Write and offer your services to help.

Most people will help if you show a serious, thoughtful, researched approach.

Think broadly
Your careers services may have vacancies for summer employment. **Voluntary work** can also be a useful way to show commitment and interest and to learn about organisations, working with people, solving problems, fund raising and organising skills.

Making it worthwhile
'I was cheap labour to them,' Simon complained. 'They wanted me to do every hour I could – and all they gave me was a £50 cheque at the end of it.'

If you don't specify what you want to get out of your work

20 Knuckleberry Wood
The Old Forest
Camptown
Farawayshire

Mr R Jones
Gregory's Wine and Cheese Store
The Mall
Greenedge, GR2 911

20 March 199X

Dear Mr Jones,

Thank you for your letter dated 14 March, in which you explained that there are no vacancies available at present.

As I mentioned to you in my letter, it is my wish to gain employment in management in the wine industry, which I believe to be an expanding one, and therefore I would be grateful if you would keep me in mind should any vacancies arise. I would also welcome any suggestions you may have as to ways in which I can strengthen my chances of success in gaining a position in your company.

I work well in a team, and have experience in training staff. I have also signed up for an introduction to wine class at our local college of further education in order that I may further improve my knowledge of wines.

I look forward to hearing from you.

Yours sincerely

J Smith (Miss)

Fig. 17. 'Keep me in mind' letter.

experience, you may find that the organisation has mundane tasks ready for you on your first day. Employers get lots of requests for work experience and it can be difficult to know what to do with people. Most would probably welcome someone who has a clear idea of what they want to get out of their work experience placement. You'll get more out of it as well. Explain what you want to achieve while there, *eg* an overview of how a business is run. Perhaps they have a project you could do.

Even if the experience is not directly relevant to the career area you want to work in, try to develop skills and competencies as listed in Chapter 2. Be willing to get involved and help others out, especially when you are not busy – and you will be noticed! Take the opportunity to ask about their recruiting methods, what others enjoy about working at the firm and what they don't, whether there are any positions available *etc*.

If you return to the same company, try to make sure you get a different sort of experience, either by working in another department or by doing more advanced work.

DEALING WITH 'NO VACANCY' AND NO RESPONSE

A frequent response to cold letters asking if a job is available is 'Sorry, but we've no vacancy at the moment.' Many firms add that they will keep your name and details on file and, should a vacancy arise in the future, they will bear you in mind.

'But what about the future?'

If you are keen on the firm, it is always worth following up such a letter with a polite response, stressing that you really are interested in and committed to joining them (see Figure 17).

Miss Smith has other options if the company has no vacancies. She could apply for a retail management position, study wines at evening classes, maintain contact with her network of employers through family, friends and colleagues and watch the job market and apply for any similar vacancies. She could do a management qualification also through distance learning to strengthen her prospects. Alternatively, she could sign up with a training programme run by the government so that she has relevant experience. She could consider starting her own business if she can find the right market niche or take on a franchise (this would require money) – though gaining experience first is advisable.

If you sent an application off and you haven't heard anything, follow up with a phone call. If you applied in response to an advert, sometimes employers may put a notice in the same paper to let everyone know that the vacancy has been filled.

Your CV may be going through a circulation process, especially if you are applying to a large firm. The right people could be away on business/pleasure, off sick, in meetings, dealing with emergencies *etc*, so these things can take time.

'Will there be a vacancy in the future?'
If you find out over the phone that the vacancy has been filled, ask if a vacancy may arise in the future and how you can strengthen your chances of getting that job.

THINKING ABOUT AGE

Questions and answers
'Will I be too old by the time I finish?'
If you are concerned about your age, you could put your date of birth at the end of your CV, thereby exciting prospective employers with the experience and skills you have to offer first.

Are there any careers which like mature people?
There are many careers where it is preferable for entrants to be older, because you bring maturity to the job and experience of life. Examples are insurance, social work, careers work and teaching.

What will employers think of my starting a degree at 40?
Many employers recognise that attending courses is one way to change a career or start afresh. They may well be impressed by your commitment and willingness to invest three years of your life in a course, while juggling other activities such as bringing up a family.

Concentrate on past work history and university course
You have lots to offer. Emphasise your stability, experience and maturity and the skills you bring in dealing with people. Some employers suggest that older people will be unable to cope with changing circumstances – you have coped with change because you moved back to full-time education.

Look at the maturity you can bring
If a team is a very young one, point out that you have studied and socialised with young people at university! Mention anything you've

done outside university which shows your ability to deal with youngsters.

You should also mention other skills and achievements, *eg* being on the PTA, budgeting the house-keeping and selecting a school.

Starting tips
- Make contact with employers early on, especially if you need to stay in the area.
- Offer your services to prove your abilities, either voluntarily or to fill in for staff who are on holiday, off sick *etc*.
- Keep in touch with past employers.
- Make a point of checking all the local papers all the time for vacancies and any news of local organisations expanding or new firms coming to the area.

Talk to your family about your next steps
If you have a family to consider, discuss your career plans with them and get their support. Work out solutions to possible problems that will worry an employer, *eg* what will happen to the kids in the holidays or when they are ill. Employers shouldn't ask you about these things, but if you bring them up yourself, it shows that you are aware they may be concerned, that you've thought ahead and solved problems before they occur.

OVERCOMING PREJUDICE

'I've got a criminal record'
Ask an employer whether they would recruit someone with a criminal record and most would say that it depends what it was for and how closely the crime relates to the work involved. This tends to be something that companies look at on an individual basis but they may have a policy, *eg* on drugs, so check early on. Early research can help and also your careers service might be able to act as a facilitator in terms of finding placements for you so that you can prove yourself. It could also be worth making greater use of appropriate government agencies who may be able to offer assistance.

Disabilities
Take action early on:
- Enlist the help of your careers service and your local TEC.

- Build up a wide network at university and back home.
- Get as much work experience as you can and use it to build up a portfolio of skills to show employers.
- Don't whinge about the difficulties of getting a job.
- Make sure you are explicit about any extra support you will need and find out as much as you can about government help – don't leave it to the employer. The more you can do to help yourself, the better.

BEING OVER-QUALIFIED

Many graduates apply for jobs for which they are over-qualified. It's often the only way into highly competitive areas, starting with work experience and showing that you can be of use to the company. If you are over-qualified for a position you're applying for, you could also write your CV and covering letter in such a way that shows you're used to dealing with the more routine parts of work and have a good appreciation of how important they are to the success of business. Show that you've handled mundane, routine tasks before and place less emphasis on your degree.

HANDLING PRESSURE

What about the competition?
You need to think about what you can offer this company that no one else can. Why should they recruit you? Put yourself in the interviewer's shoes. What can you tell him that makes you stand out above everyone else?

Responding to family and friends
Their constant questions about your future might drive you mad, but friends and family are just interested in what you're going to do and they care. They want you to do well. Some of them have probably invested a lot of time and interest in guiding you and helping you along the way. Enlist their help – ask them to send local papers and recruitment pages, together with information about local companies.

'I told you you wouldn't automatically get a job'
If people are being negative, try to avoid them. They might be going through difficult times of their own for some reason. Right now, you

Dealing with the bank manager

In debt? Most students are in debt by the end of their degree course, but at the same time, graduate salaries are starting to rise. Talk to your bank about paying your overdraft or loans off – remember that most want to keep your custom. If problems arise, let the bank know so that you can at least try to work out a solution. Budget for work as well – working costs money! Some banks will give you a special loan *eg* for an interview outfit.

FINDING IT HARD TO GET A PLACEMENT

If you are studying for a profession where a period of work experience is compulsory in order to qualify, it is sometimes not possible to find a placement, perhaps because business is slack. Check the options with your professional body but two possibilities for coping with a lack of a placement include:

1. Doing two short placements with different employers instead of one long one. Employers may feel more confident about offering people a placement for a short period of time.
2. Working for a firm abroad to fulfil the requirement.

Michael goes down under

Michael studied architecture but had trouble finding a year's placement to continue his training. A family friend in Australia suggested that he go out to Sydney for a year and join his practice there. He did, checking first with his professional body that this would be satisfactory, and then enjoyed the benefits of a year abroad while continuing working for his qualifications.

SUMMARY

- Persistence may pay off so keep trying.
- Get feedback to improve your interview technique.
- Check other routes into careers you really want – there are often other ways in.
- Don't give up hope: many people are in the same boat.

CASE STUDIES

Sarah starts work
Her first day was strange – Sarah didn't know anyone and she got the impression the other staff resented her. 'They look down their noses at me just because I've got a degree,' she told Marion. Marion advised Sarah to join in all the office activities – joining the lottery syndicate, going out socially, making tea for others as well as herself – and to do her job well. Gradually, Sarah found that these tactics were working and she made good friends with the other staff members as they accepted her.

Matthew gets advice
Matthew was rejected and he rang the company to ask for feedback. 'You didn't have much work experience,' the personnel manager told him after also explaining that his lack of research had not, they thought, demonstrated a natural interest in the job. Matthew called the local TEC for help. They put him in touch with a small PR company. Matthew phoned ahead for company information, and sent a letter and CV to the managing director, asking for 20 minutes of his time to discuss ways to get into the PR career. The MD agreed to meet with him briefly. 'We'll let you know if we have anything,' he was told.

Mary meets barriers at home
Mary was offered the job, but met with resentment and anger from her husband. 'Thought the degree was enough,' he sniffed. He wanted her at home doing the ironing. Mary spent a lot of time talking through her thoughts with Bob and made sure that they had some time to spend on their own while talking about their future. Gradually, she won him round.

DISCUSSION POINTS

1. How seriously should you take employment statistics? How do they affect you?

2. How important is age as a criteria for selection?

3. If you meet with race or sex discrimination when applying for a job, which bodies might be able to help you? How can they help?

9
Coping with Unemployment or Underemployment

EXPECTING IT

Many graduates won't get straight into the job that they want. You may find that it takes a couple of years to find the right job, partly because by then, you've had more experience of work and you will probably find that your initial thoughts and wishes change as you learn more about yourself, develop at work and the employment market alters.

It can take time to find a job

You won't necessarily find a job immediately after finishing university, especially if you don't/didn't start looking until late in your final year. In 1992 for example, some twelve per cent of graduates were still unemployed six months after finishing their degrees. Plus many recruitment procedures take ages, especially in big organisations. Smaller employers may wait to see how business prospects are looking before they commit to taking on extra staff.

That term-time feeling

September/October is a strange time for people who've left full-time education. Everyone else goes back to meet up after the holidays, talk about the work to be done that term...and you're not. If you haven't got a job, you can feel more lost still, because you can easily find yourself without structure and routine. Friends and family aren't used to you being around at this time of year, either!

Coping

It's not easy being unemployed:

Paul avoids ringing home
Paul graduated from university with a chemistry degree. His first interviews did not go well and he moved in with a friend who was

working and willing to put him up while he looked for a job. When Paul rang home, his mother always asked 'How's the job situation? Oh well, never mind, it's very difficult to find work these days.' Paul stopped ringing home: he found these conversations increasingly difficult to handle. 'I'll ring them when I've got good news,' he decided.

BEING SINGLE-MINDED

'Anything will do, I just want a job'

If you aren't getting positive responses from your first few applications, it's easy to start saying to yourself, 'Well, I'll apply for anything', out of sheer desperation. And that's when you start hitting a vicious circle, as Figure 18 illustrates.

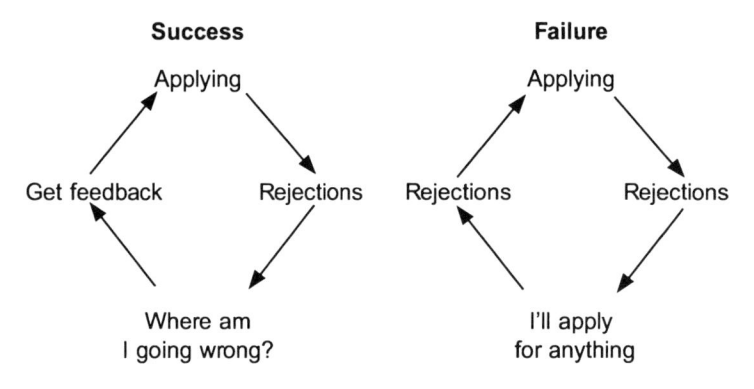

Fig. 18. Virtuous and vicious circles.

Employers get nervous of people who apply for just anything, because it displays lack of commitment and self-confidence. You could look for a position which is at a lower level in the career area you want, just to get in there, but do think ahead and make sure you are acquiring relevant skills.

KEEPING BUSY

Applying for work can be a full-time job!

You can easily spend 35 hours a week looking for a job:

- checklist places to look for work every week
- call your contacts every two weeks
- get relevant work experience

Coping with Unemployment or Underemployment

- learn new skills
- visit your local TEC, Jobcentre
- attend anything that will bring you into contact with others – you're networking.

Discipline yourself
Stick to a **regular routine**. If you stay in bed until lunchtime, you won't feel like doing anything when you get up. It will also be more difficult to explain your period of inactivity to a future employer.

Keep fit
It doesn't have to cost much to keep fit and in shape – which in itself disciplines the mind, keeps you alert and gives you goals to work for. Running, walking, swimming and cycling are all easy to enjoy and can cost very little.

Keep your mind active
- keep updated with local, national and international events
- pursue interests and hobbies
- do voluntary work
- learn new skills, *eg* a language (libraries may have tapes to borrow).

GETTING THERE...BY HOOK OR BY CROOK

Temping times
Temporary staff are needed constantly by firms to cover for:

- sickness
- holiday
- people leaving without a replacement
- extra work loads
- maternity leave
- absences due to bereavements *etc*.

Why not fill in?

Pros
Temping can:

- provide you with money on a weekly basis
- give you further insight into the world of work
- lead to more work with the same company

- enable you to move around firms finding out what you want from a career
- be in a variety of sectors, *eg* media, public relations
- be useful in university holidays
- be well paid
- help in paying off the overdraft
- increase your network – you're meeting people who have their own network.

Cons
- you can't be guaranteed work
- it's rare to have holiday or sick pay – on any days off, *eg* bank holidays – you may lose out financially
- it can easily turn into a long-term placement which is hard to move out of.

But remember
- Be willing to turn your hand to *anything*.
- Arrive early and offer to stay late.
- Ask others if you can help them if you run out of things to do – don't sit with nothing to do.
- Look the part and watch your image.
- Don't turn placements down unless you have a good reason.
- Join in any social events: colleagues may introduce you to their contacts!
- Expect to have the easier tasks to do – you're there to fill in.
- Look cheerful and be helpful so people want to have you around the place!

Making use of training schemes
Government training schemes can provide you with a good foot in the door and although they won't be that well paid, they will provide you with a wealth of experience, more contacts and a good reference. They could even lead to full-time employment. Your local TEC can help – some offer programmes specifically for graduates.

Check to make sure that you have a good understanding of the government schemes available in your area, not only those assigned to help people who are unemployed but also those which help people who want to, for example, start their own business.

Many Jobcentres and TECs also run courses called 'Jobsearch Plus' or 'Job Search' offering advice and help to people who are having difficulties finding work. In some cases, you have to be unemployed for a certain length of time.

Getting in at a lower level

You may have to take a lower level job, despite all your efforts to secure something else.

Competitive, popular careers

If you want work in a competitive and popular career and are offered a lower level job than you wanted, don't pass it by. Accepting it shows commitment and it will give you a foot in the door, a chance to prove your worth and to network. Make it your goal to see how different your CV will look between joining and moving on. Select the person who is in the post you want and find out how they succeeded. People love to give advice and talk about their 'lucky break'.

A starting point

You may have taken a full-time 'permanent' job because you could find nothing else. If this is the case, you could use it as a stepping stone while you are looking for something more worthwhile – at least you are earning some money – or use it to show what you can do, through various methods as outlined below.

Is it going to be like this all the time?

You may be given time to settle in and see how you adapt and cope with the easier tasks first. Complete the tasks you are given well and ask if you can take on the more demanding ones. Again, talk to your supervisor, manager or personnel staff to see what you can do to move forward. There may be another vacancy within the organisation to which you could move across. You don't have to stay in the same section.

You are not alone

Many people at work feel underemployed. Don't wait for the organisation to do something about it. Put yourself forward and take on more tasks (perhaps ask your boss to delegate something to you).

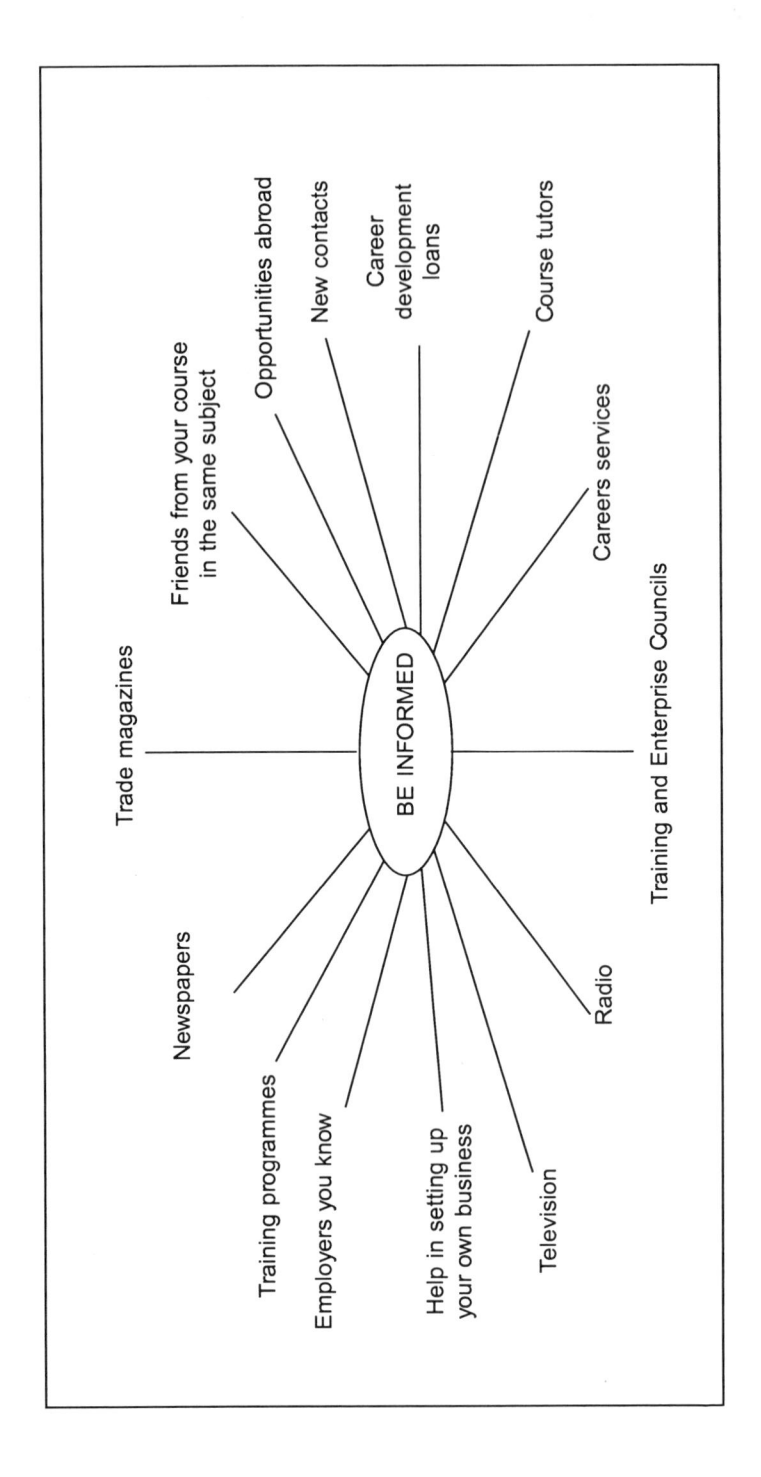

Fig. 19. Avenues to information.

The experience may catch up with you later
Lower level work can provide useful knowledge and understanding of what it is like to be doing menial work – you're more likely to empathise with junior staff when promoted to a supervisory or management position yourself. If you are on a temporary contract, mention that you are looking for permanent work and see if the firm can help. If you are good, they will want to keep you.

KEEPING THE JOB MARKET IN MIND

Experience first please
Some firms want you to have a couple of years' experience first, *eg* with people if you want to be a counsellor, so build up a good knowledge of what they might want from you during those two years in terms of skills, abilities and experience and then go out to get them. Keep in touch with your contacts.

Some firms deliberately recruit graduates with one or two years' experience, thereby giving them the chance to develop and prove themselves. They choose to pick up people who want to change and have gained work experience as well as some initial training.

Information is power
- read
- network
- listen and look.

See Figure 19 for ways of gathering information.

Track your experience and development
Careers are like building blocks. You lay your foundations in full-time education and then begin adding blocks of experience and self-knowledge. Each building block should add something new to your portfolio of skills and work history. This will require continuous effort from you as you keep up to date with employment trends and labour market demands on skills.

Training outside work
There's an extensive range of courses available, and you may be able to acquire a Career Development Loan or some financial assistance from a Training and Enterprise Council. Visit your TEC to see what's available in your area, what financial assistance you might be able to acquire, and make a training plan. It will provide evidence of your commitment to a particular career area and help you in the job market.

SUMMARY

- Keep thinking and planning ahead to make sure you plug any skill gaps.
- Watch the job market all the time and make sure you know who can help you find the work you want.
- Network – keep in touch with your contacts even when you have got a job.

CASE STUDIES

Sarah's contract ends
Sarah found that her new job wasn't challenging her enough. She was relieved it was just for one year. 'I'll stay here and complete the contract and move on,' she thought. Two months before her contract ended, her boss pushed an advert under her nose. 'Why don't you apply for this?' he asked. It was an Arts Administrator post – organising a programme of events for the local arts theatre. Sarah jumped at the chance and applied.

Matthew uses the Internet
Matthew was unemployed. He tried to keep active and not worry, but it was difficult because he didn't want to disappoint his parents or himself. Surfing the Internet recruitment pages, he saw an advert by the same small company whose MD he'd seen back in his university town. He e-mailed his CV straight to him with a covering letter. The firm called him back the next day. 'Come and see us,' they said.

Mary gets fully involved
Mary's day-time involvement with young mothers soon spread to two nights a week at the local youth centre as a voluntary helper. Her talent with young people was quickly spotted by the local youth officer, who admired her enthusiasm and energy. 'I'm forming a group to tackle drugs,' he told her one week. 'Would you like to join us? We could do with people like you.' Mary leapt at the chance.

DISCUSSION POINTS

1. What immediate help is available to those in your area who are unemployed?

2. What are the main reasons for people being out of work in your area?

10
The Route to Being Employed

STARTING WORK

You've been offered the job! You celebrate and read the letter several times. You may have been offered two or three jobs – in which case you'll need to decide which lucky employer is to have your services. It may be a good time to talk this over with your careers adviser. Sometimes you know instinctively which employer you want to join. you accept a package and agree a start date. How can you make an impact?

Preparing for Day One
- Aim to arrive well rested, fit and healthy and appropriately dressed.
- Expect to be nervous – you're starting another chapter in your life!
- Check travel times to get there.
- Eat a good breakfast before you start to give you energy.
- Take any necessary documents with you, such as bank account details.
- Prepare your clothes the night before

What will the first few days be like?
Starting work is like arriving in a foreign country, knowing few people, if any, and not quite knowing what to do, where to go and yet feeling you should be able to fit straight in. There'll be a lot to pick up, so give yourself time to settle in. Don't be surprised if you feel confused at first.

If you are starting work with a large firm, there may be a meeting of all those who are just beginning with the company, to welcome you and take you through an **induction programme**. If you are with a small one, you may find that you are expected to start working at once.

At last... a pay cheque!
Working costs money! You'll need money for clothes, transport to and from work, national insurance, tax, lunch, socialising with colleagues, food and lodging. Budget for any loans or overdrafts you have to pay back.

A month in arrears
Most firms pay people one month in arrears – so your first month could mean you have virtually no money to spend.

Paperwork
If you have previously been employed, you will need your P45. If you do not know your national insurance number, call your local Social Security office. You employer will need the number so that you can get state benefits. If you haven't worked before, you'll have to fill in a P46 form – which should be supplied by the company. This gives you your own tax code (you may be issued with an emergency one if you are starting work very quickly).

Paying off your debts
Banks are putting considerable efforts into smoothing graduates' movement into work. Many have graduate accounts which extend your interest-free overdraft. After all, they want your custom in the future. Talk to the Student Loan Company and let them know of any change in address.

Pensions
Invest in a private pension if your company does not offer you one. Talk to an independent financial adviser about taking out a personal pension from an insurance company or bank if your company does not operate a pension scheme. Don't leave it till later. It's never too early to start investing in a pension scheme.

Saving money for opportunities
What if you suddenly decided you wanted to start your own business? Or buy into a franchise operation? Or go travelling for the year? Try to put money aside after you've paid off your debts: you can face turbulent times at work more confidently.

PREPARING FOR YOUR FUTURE

You should have discussed your future with the company at the interview stage and talked to other employees to see how they have progressed.

Acquiring your passport to continual employment
Keep a career file at home and add details of your achievements, new skills, training courses *etc* regularly. When the time comes to move on to a new job, you will be in a better position to look back through your career and explain to a prospective new employer how you made a difference to your organisation and to your CV.

Develop your skills base
Think of your career as a set of building blocks. As you put extra blocks on to your foundations (*ie* your previous history), via new job, new position, new responsibility, perhaps new company, you add skills, experience, qualifications and qualities. As you move into your career, things like GCSEs and further education results become less important. Even if your job disappears, you will still have your skills base.

Enough is enough
There will come a time when you know it's time to move on, even if your job is safe from redundancy. You start to outgrow your work, it's no longer challenging and you want to progress. You could:

- delegate easier tasks so you can take new projects on
- look to move up or sideways in your organisation
- move out.

Keep an eye on the job market and an ear to the ground. You may decide for example that you want to change career.

Sandra seeks a change of career
Sandra trained and then worked as a physiotherapist. She wanted a change, although she liked teaching her patients the exercises they had to do at home and enjoyed seeing their confidence develop. She trained to become a teacher and now teaches Biology. She transferred her skills with people, her knowledge of the sciences and her interest in helping others to a new career.

Staying in work
1. Make yourself a valuable member of the organisation, *eg* be a good team member, support and help other members of staff, be professional and do your job well. Get yourself known as someone

who makes things happen. Be aware of office politics which could impact on you and your department. Ask yourself how future changes are likely to impact your section. Promote change, initiate new ideas, get involved.

2. Be flexible – the workplace is changing too fast for job descriptions to keep up so don't refuse to do something just because your description does not include it.

3. Always add value to your CV. Can you look back over one year's work and say that it is different from the previous year? Take responsibility for your own career development – don't leave it to your employer. You may have different ideas about where you want to go, after all! Keep your CV at home – primed and ready for action.

4. Know about the events that could impact on your company, developments in your specific area of work, and the job market. Be prepared to change jobs or organisations if it is the right thing for you to do. Know when it is time for you to move on – even if it means changing organisations.

5. Excel at what you do and care about your image and that of your company. Market yourself, not just in job hunting but every day. You never know – clients you meet could be so impressed by your image, personality and skills that they ask you to join them.

6. Think ahead: know where you want to go and what you need to get there, so that you can make sure you are prepared to make the move.

LEARNING: WILL IT NEVER END?

It's a lifelong process now
Knowledge becomes outdated rapidly today. Technology has a short life span. The quest in a competitive environment is to produce something better, faster, more professional, cheaper and of good value. You will always need training to keep up with it all.

Training methods are flexible
Government efforts to encourage more organisations and individuals to train, mean that the opportunities to do so are increasingly varied (see Figure 20).

Continuing professional development
Would you want to visit a doctor who was out of date with all the changes and developments that had taken place within the field of medicine? Many professions now incorporate a requirement for Continuing Professional Development, in which they state that a certain number of hours or days a year must be given over to training and development, so that their members can keep up to date with advances and new techniques.

Don't get stale
Just as a company strives to keep ahead of its competitors, so you need to keep ahead in your skills, knowledge and attitude, even if you do it in your spare time. Staying still means losing ground.

People who are comfortable at work find it hardest to cope with change. They resist change because they fear learning anything new or it takes too much effort. They are concerned about the effect change will have on their jobs. But companies must respond to customer needs and external factors, or they wouldn't survive, so jobs which stay the same aren't doing the organisation a favour. Learn to move with change and see it as a positive force.

REDUNDANCY – WILL IT HAPPEN TO ME?

Employers need a flexible workforce
Job security does not exist any more. Even in Japan, where employers pride themselves on giving people jobs for life, companies find it is increasingly difficult to do this and are resorting to methods such as redeploying employees to other firms.

Dealing with it
Imagine that you are made redundant. What would you do? How would you cope? Would you be ready to go job hunting? If you are ready to be made redundant, it is easier to deal with it should it happen.

Nicky makes the most of her skills, abilities and networking
Nicky graduated in Economics and got a job in sales and marketing with a big hotel chain. She was made redundant when it reduced staffing levels and, with the redundancy money, she travelled for nine months. She returned to Britain and found a new job in sales and marketing for a tour operator.

Nicky was qualified and excelled at her work. She had good

Training = increased job prospects

via

Day-release courses

Work shadowing

Work experience

Project work

Short courses

Distance learning courses

Block courses

Part-time

Evening classes

Secondments

Mentoring

Assessment in the workplace

On-the-job training

Degree courses related to work, *eg* MBAs

Exchange programmes

Short lectures

Finding out by doing

Research projects

Continued professional development

Reading relevant material

Coaching

If the company does not offer you training, invest in your own.

It will pay dividends.

Fig. 20. Training means increased job prospects.

networks and got advice from friends and colleagues. She saw redundancy as an opportunity, *eg* to have a break.

Making the most of it
Redundancy is a terrible shock. But it can start you out on a new track, taking skills, experience and qualifications with you. After the initial shock and disbelief, there are still those who say 'Redundancy is the best thing that could have happened to me'.

Jenny adjusts to changing circumstances
Jenny graduated in Graphic Design and worked in publishing. After four years, she took a career break and travelled for six months. By the time she came home, the job market had changed completely and Jenny couldn't find a job anywhere. So she set up her own business aided by government-run self-employment schemes.

SUMMARY

- Use change to create opportunity.
- Keep a career passport at home.
- Network to maintain a high profile.
- Be informed.
- Keep doing your SWOT update, *ie*:
  - analyse your Strengths
  - analyse your Weaknesses
  - identify Opportunities
  - identify Threats
  and take appropriate action!
- Don't let fear of success stand in your way.

Being good isn't good enough. You have to be better. If you have the right attitude and drive, you can be.

CASE STUDIES

Sarah enjoys her job but should look forward
Sarah excelled in her new job. She enjoyed negotiating deals with artists' agents, promoting shows, pricing tickets and planning the year's programme. She was on radio often, promoting the theatre's

activities. 'I'm happy now,' she told Marion. 'I love my job.' 'It won't be enough in five years' time,' Marion told her. 'What are you going to do next?' Sarah didn't know. 'I'd better give it some thought,' she said.

Matthew starts at a low level

Matthew spent the 24 hours before his interview preparing for it. 'We've just been given a huge new account,' the MD told him. 'We need someone to do the donkey work – it's all basic, but it's a start. If you're good, we'll train you. Can you start next Monday? If you're as energetic as your CV says you are, you'll do well with us – we need doers.' Matthew started on Monday.

Mary finds her niche

Mary was asked to take on extra responsibilities as people realised how effective she was. Later she was asked to apply for a management post. 'No thanks,' Mary said. 'This is what I want to do, helping youngsters as individuals. Management will take me away from that.' Mary's choice, Mary's decision.

DISCUSSION POINTS

1. What worries you most about starting work? How can you alleviate those worries?

2. How can you plan for retirement? What sorts of activities are retired people becoming involved with?

3. What are you looking forward to most about your future?

GOOD LUCK!

Glossary

Action planning. Setting a goal and breaking it down into achievable bits. Action planning gives you a series of targets to aim for by certain deadlines, *eg* prepare CV by Tuesday.

Attitude. A passion for something which makes you want to excel, to provide outstanding service, to have pride in what you are doing and whom you are representing, someone others can rely on, who will get things done in positive fashion while responding to changing priorities.

Business Link. A nationwide business support partnership of TECs, Chambers of Commerce, local authorities and enterprise agencies designed to offer a fast route to a range of information and advice available.

Career planning. Identifying what you want in your career and planning how you'll get there.

Closed questions. Rarely asked in interviews by experienced interviewers since they can be answered with a simple 'yes' or 'no', *eg* 'Did you enjoy...?' They are useful for quietening candidates who waffle as they do not encourage the applicant to talk. They may also be used by the interviewer to check understanding or to get a quick answer.

Computer literacy. Understanding what computers can do and their potential impact. Knowing how to use them beyond the basic keyboard stage and to use them as a way to communicate with others.

Continued professional development. Frequently required by the professions in order to keep their members up to date with change, *eg* in law, technology *etc*. Some professions demand that members must have *eg* 35 hours of training a year.

Customer care. Making a customer feel special, looking after your client so that he goes away happy with the service that he has received (and is more likely to come back again). Never mind the 100 others who are also in your careful hands.

Decision-making. The skills used to make a decision about something, *eg* your career. To make an informed realistic decision about your career, you need **self-awareness, opportunity awareness** and **transition skills**.

Image. The way you project yourself to others. They will learn a lot about you by your appearance, the way you talk to people, the way you handle them, your behaviour and attitude. Your image speaks volumes about you!

Jargon. Language known and understood only by those connected with that subject which needs explaining to everyone else.

JobSite. An organisation that gives you access, via the Internet, to a whole range of agencies and job vacancies to which you can then apply via e-mail. This makes job-hunting a much quicker exercise.

Lateral thinking. Looking at a situation broadly, so that your options increase and you have more choice.

National Vocational Qualifications (NVQs). NVQs provide a framework of qualifications for a very wide variety of careers. They are assessed at work and are divided into units, so for example, a unit in Supervisory Management may mean that you are assessed in a number of situations in performing staff appraisals or taking a meeting.

Open questions. Questions asked that require more than a simple 'yes' or 'no' answer, *eg* 'How did you cope with...?' 'What is important...?' They are frequently used in interviews to encourage applicants to talk.

Opportunity awareness. Knowing the opportunities in education, employment and training that are available to you and knowing how they match your skills, strengths and interests.

PeopleBank. The Employment Network which offers employers a new, fast, efficient and cost-effective way to recruit staff, using the Internet. Employers can access a database of candidates. Candidates have a fast and free route to employment.

Portfolio worker. Someone who has two or three jobs at once.

Recruitment agency. A commercial organisation which seeks people to fill vacant posts on behalf of employers. The positions available may be short or long term and some recruitment agencies specialise in a career area.

Self-awareness. A vital key to successful career decision-making. Knowledge about yourself: your interests, skills, strengths, weaknesses, values, needs, potential and ambition.

Skills base. Your skills base consists of those skills you enjoy using the most and are best with, *eg* communicating for a radio announcer.

Although you may change jobs, your skills base stays with you – and gets better and more effective!

TECs. Training and Enterprise Councils have been established on a regional basis throughout the UK to assist economic growth and ensure that the workforce is skilled and flexible. TECs work closely with local business organisations and have a thorough knowledge of employment opportunities in their local areas.

Temping. A slang term for 'temporary work', whereby the 'temp' goes to work for successive organisations, usually sent by a recruitment agency.

Time management. Making the most of your time, prioritising your workload and meeting deadlines.

Transferable skills. Skills that are common to many jobs and which you can transfer from one job to another. For example, Study Abroad Adviser (communicating, facilitating, enabling, advising, counselling) to Careers Officer (ditto).

Transition making. Making the transition, *eg* from school to university or university to work. This involves the whole process of applying for courses or jobs. Transition skills will be vital as jobs increasingly tend to be for shorter periods of time or on a contract basis.

Useful Addresses

British Franchise Association, Thames View, New Town Road, Henley-on-Thames, Oxfordshire RG7 1HG.

Careers Service (local) – check *Yellow Pages*.

Colour Me Beautiful, Freepost, London SW8 3NS. Tel: (0171) 627 5211. Will advise on colours which suit you best to enhance your image.

Community Service Volunteers, 237 Pentonville Road, London N1 9NJ.

CSU Ltd, Armstrong House, Oxford Road, Manchester M1 7ED. Tel: (0161) 236 9816. CSU produce a wide range of booklets on careers for graduates, many of which are available at your university careers service.

Employment Service, Overseas Placing Unit, 4th Floor, Steel City House, Moorfoot, Sheffield, South Yorkshire S1 4PQ.

The Federation of Recruitment and Employment Services Ltd (FRES), 36/38 Mortimer Street, London W1N 7RB.

JobSite UK (Worldwide) Ltd: http://www.jobsite@.co.uk (for vacancies); alternatively, send an e-mail to jobsite@jobsite.co.uk requesting the type of work sought.

LiveWIRE, Freepost NT805, Newcastle Upon Tyne NE1 1BR or call 0345 573252 (local call charge). Relevant to 16–26-year-olds who wish to start their own business. Offers information and a range of services to help.

National Association for the Care and Resettlement of Offenders (NACRO), National Education Advisory Service, 567 Barlow Moor Road, Manchester M21 2AE. Information and advice on colleges, courses and grants.

Opportunities for the Disabled, 1 Bank Building, Prince's Street, London EC2R 8EU. Tel: (0171) 726 4963. Counselling, job search and guidance on training opportunities.

PeopleBank – the Employment Network, Harmsworth Quay Press, Surrey Quays Road, London SE16 1PJ. Tel: 0800 200220. E-mail:

register@peoplebank.com. Internet Home Page at http://www.peoplebank.com.

Skill: National Bureau for Students with Disabilities, 336 Brixton Road, London SW9 7AA. Tel: (0171) 274 0565. Helps those with disabilities or learning difficulties.

Student Loans Company Ltd, 100 Bothwell Street, Glasgow G2 7JD.

TECs: Training and Enterprise Councils – check *Yellow Pages*.

Training Access Points (TAPs), St Mary's House, c/o Moorfoot, Sheffield S1 4PQ.

Further Reading

MAKING PLANS

Managing Yourself, Julie-Ann Amos (How To Books Ltd, 1996).
Writing Your Dissertation, Derek Swetnam (How To Books Ltd, 2nd edition 1997).
The Job Hunter's Handbook, David Greenwood (Kogan Page, 1995).

TAKING STOCK

How to Master Public Speaking, Anne Nicholls (How To Books Ltd, 1995).
Test your Own Aptitude, J Barrett and G Williams (Kogan Page, 1990).
What Color is Your Parachute? Richard Nelson Bolles (Ten Speed Press, 1996).

GETTING IN TOUCH WITH REALITY

Finding a Job with a Future, Laurel Alexander (How To Books Ltd, 1996).
What Do Graduates Do? (CRAC Annual).
The POSTGRAD Series: The Directory of Graduate Studies, 1996/97, CRAC *Casebooks 1997* (CRAC) contains graduate profiles which offer students an insight into the qualifications and qualities you need to work in various careers.
Graduate, Employment and Training (GET) (Hobsons, CRAC, DPA) lists vacancies and graduate courses, available in most careers libraries plus on the Internet: http://www.hobsons.co.uk.
The Prospects Series (graduate employer directories) available from CSU Ltd, or in your university careers service library.
The Distance Learning Guide (CRAC) includes details about postgraduate distance learning programmes.
Occupations, 1997 (Careers Occupation and Information centre,

annual).
The Times 1000: the definitive reference to businesses.
Kompass, the authority on British industry (libraries have a copy). Covers industrial trade names, financial data and products and services.
Graduate Opportunities in Singapore (CSU Ltd).

ESTABLISHING YOUR NEEDS AND VALUES

Build your own Rainbow, A Workbook for Career and Life Management, Barrie Hopson and Mike Scally (Mercury Books, 1995).
How to Work from Home Ian Phillipson (How To Books Ltd, 1995).

SHOWING YOU'VE GOT THE RIGHT ATTITUDE

The Image Factor, Eleri Sampson (Kogan Page, 1994).
Developing Self-Esteem, Connie D. Palladino (Kogan Page, 1996).
Assert Yourself, Robert Sharpe (Kogan Page, 1995).

LOOKING FOR WORK

Doing Voluntary Work Abroad, Mark Hempshell (How To Books Ltd, 2nd edition, 1997).
Finding a Job with a Future, Laurel Alexander (How To Books, 1996).
Finding Work Overseas, Matthew Cunningham (How To Books Ltd, 1996).
How to Get a Job Abroad, Roger Jones (How To Books Ltd, 1996).
How to Start Your Own Business, Jim Green (How To Books Ltd, 1995).
How to Use the Internet, Graham Jones (How To Books Ltd, 1996).
Guide to Stages: An Introduction to Work Experience in Europe for Students and Graduates, J. A. Goodman (CSU Ltd, 1996).
Working in the European Union: a Guide for Graduate Recruiters and Job-seekers, W. H. Archer and A. J. Raban (Office for Official Publications of the European Community and Hobsons Publishing plc, 1995).
First Steps to Working in Europe, AGCAS Careers Information Booklet, 1996.
Summer Jobs in Britain (Vacation Work, Oxford).
Summer Jobs Abroad (Vacation Work, Oxford).

MARKETING YOURSELF

How to Write a Curriculum Vitae (University of London Careers Service).
Preparing Your Own CV, Rebecca Corfield (Kogan Page, 1990).
Great Answers to Tough Interview Questions, Martin John Yate (Kogan Page, 1992).
How to Pass Graduate Recruitment Tests, Mike Byron (Kogan Page, 1994).
How to Pass Numeracy Tests, Harry Tolley and Ken Thomas (Kogan Page, 1996).
How to Pass Verbal Reasoning Tests, Harry Tolley and Ken Thomas (Kogan Page, 1996).
How to Pass the Civil Service Qualifying Tests, Mike Bryon (Kogan Page, 1995).
How to Pass Computer Selection Tests, Sanjay Modha (Kogan Page, 1994).
Writing a CV That Works, Paul McGee (How To Books Ltd, 2nd edition, 1997).
How to Apply for a Job, Judith Johnstone (How To Books Ltd, 2nd edition, 1994).

OVERCOMING OBSTACLES AND BARRIERS

Equal Opportunities (CRAC): Disabled Graduates and their Careers.
Feel the fear and do it anyway, Susan Jeffers (Arrow Books Ltd, 1987).

THE ROUTE TO BEING EMPLOYED

Understanding Your Rights at Work, Robert Spicer (How To Books Ltd, 3rd edition, 1997).
How to Market Yourself, Ian Phillipson (How To Books Ltd, 1995).
How to Manage your Personal Finances, John Claxton (How To Books Ltd, 1996).
Employability, Susan Bloch and Terence Bates (Kogan Page, 1995).

Index

Achievements, 15, 24, 27, 61
Action planning, 19, 20, 64, 131
Added value, 32, 33, 92
Age, 110-111
Application forms, 93, 96
Assessment centres, 102-104
Attitude, 61-68, 131

Books, 75
Business awareness, 27

Career choice, 16, 30, 37-44
Careers counsellor, 21
Career management file, 25, 126
Career planning, 12, 13, 131
Careers conventions, 81
Careers services, 21, 22
Changing career, 18, 125
Competing, 37, 41, 112
Contract work, 37, 83
Criminal record, 111
CVs, 77, 88-93, 94-95, 125, 126

Department, 52
Disability, 112

Excitement, 11
Expectation, 17
Experience, 13-14, 18, 92, 110, 121

Fear, 11, 19

Feeling lost, 115
Finding information, 14, 21, 69-85, 120
Flexible workforce, 37
Franchise, 59, 83

Good news, 11, 69

Holidays, 13, 14, 22

Image, 61, 65-67, 142
Independence, 57
Internet, 73
Inter-railing, 28
Interview technique, 97-102

Job competition, 41
Job market, 121
Job security, 11
JobSite, 73, 132

Lack of work experience, 106-107, 108, 109
Letters, 77-78, 89-90, 108
Libraries, 74
Location, 51

Managing, 25
Messages, 11
Milkround, 82
Money, 55, 113, 124

Networking, 13, 14, 69-72, 76
Network marketing, 58
Newspapers, 75

Over-qualified, 112

Passion, 62, 92
Pension, 124
PeopleBank, 73, 74, 132
Perks, 56, 57
Personal touch, 34, 36
Placements, 113
Planning ahead, 14
Portfolio person, 58, 132
Positive thinking, 85
Potential, 31, 32
Presentations, 81, 104
Professional bodies, 76
Promotion, 49

Recruitment agencies, 79-81, 132
Redundancy, 127-129
Referees, 93
Rejected, 106
Response, none, 109

Saving time, 12, 15
Selection methods, 102-104
Self-awareness, 132
Size, 51

Skills, 24-33, 36, 125, 132
Small firms, 44
Specialising, 50, 51
Starting work, 123
Stress, 17
Success, 47

TECs, 13, 22, 44, 57, 72, 76, 117-118, 121, 132
Temporary work, 14, 79, 117-118, 132
Television, 74
Time out, 54
Training, 52, 121, 126-127
Training methods, 128
Training schemes, 118-119, 121
Transferable skills, 14, 24-31, 32

Underemployed, 115-122
Unemployed, 14, 115-122
Using information technology, 73
Using the media, 73, 74
Using the telephone, 85, 97-98

Wasting time, 13
When to apply, 42, 69
Work experience, 14
Working abroad, 55, 83-84
Working for yourself, 57-58, 82, 83

APPLYING FOR A JOB
How to sell your skills and experience to a prospective employer

Judith Johnstone

Tough new realities have hit the jobs market. It is no longer enough to send employers mass-produced letters and CVs with vague details of 'hobbies and interests'. Employers want to know: 'What skills have you got? How much personal commitment? Will it be worth training you longer term?' Whether you are a school or college leaver, a mature returner, out of work or facing redundancy, this book shows you step-by-step how to tackle job applications, how to decide what you are really offering, and how to sell this effectively to your future employer. The latest edition has been further revised and updated. 'Very practical and informative.' *Phoenix/Association of Graduate Careers Advisory Services.* Judith Johnstone is a qualified local government administrator and Member of the Institute of Personnel & Training. She has written extensively on employment topics.

160pp, illus. 1 85703 325 6. 3rd edition.

FINDING A JOB WITH A FUTURE
How to identify and work in growth industries and services

Laurel Alexander

Are you seeking to change your career? Have you been made redundant? Are you returning to work? If you want to ensure a long lasting career move in the right direction, you need to read this book which sets out in a practical way, growth areas of industry and commerce. Discover the work cycle of the future based on job specific skills, abstract skills, continuous learning and life-time career planning. Learn about flexible ways of working. There is occupational information on IT, training and education, business services, leisure, the entertainment industry, social and cultural fields, security and protective services, science and working for the environment. There are job and personal self assessments for each section, plus where to go for training and how to find the jobs. Laurel Alexander is a manager/trainer in career development who has helped many individuals succeed in changing their work direction.

144pp, illus. 1 85703 310 8.

GETTING YOUR FIRST JOB
How to win the offer of good prospects and a regular pay packet

Penny Hitchin

It's a tough world for jobhunters – especially for those with no track record. The days when newcomers to the job market could walk into 'A job for life' have gone. Jobseekers today must impress a potential employer with their personal qualities and attitudes as well as their paper qualifications. Once in work, they must show themselves to be willing, adaptable and flexible – able to learn new skills quickly and cope with constant change. This readable handbook offers young people a real insight into what employers are looking for, encouraging the reader to take a constructive and positive approach to finding their first job. The book includes lots of practical examples, self-assessment material and typical case studies. Penny Hitchin has run Jobfinder programmes and written careers books and materials for TV and radio campaigns on training and employment.

128pp, illus. 1 85703 300 0.

PASSING THAT INTERVIEW
Your step-by-step guide to achieving success

Judith Johnstone

Everyone knows how to shine at interview – or do they? When every candidate becomes the perfect clone of the one before, you have to have that extra 'something' to raise your chances above the rest. Using a systematic and practical approach, this How To book takes you step-by-step through the essential pre-interview groundwork, the interview encounter itself, and what you can learn from the experience afterwards. The book contains sample pre- and post-interview correspondence, and is complete with a guide to further reading, glossary of terms, and index. 'This is from the first class How To Books stable.' *Escape Committee Newsletter.* 'Offers a fresh approach to a well documented subject.' *Newscheck/Careers Service Bulletin.* 'A complete step-by-step guide.' *The Association of Business Executives.* Judith Johnstone is a Graduate of the Institute of Personnel & Development; she has been an instructor in Business Studies and adult literacy tutor, and has long experience of helping people at work.

144pp, illus. 1 85703 360 4. 4th edition.

How To Books

How To Books provide practical help on a large range of topics. They are available through all good bookshops or can be ordered direct from the distributors. Just tick the titles you want and complete the form on the following page.

- ___ Apply to an Industrial Tribunal (£7.99)
- ___ Applying for a Job (£8.99)
- ___ Applying for a United States Visa (£15.99)
- ___ Backpacking Round Europe (£8.99)
- ___ Be a Freelance Journalist (£8.99)
- ___ Be a Freelance Secretary (£8.99)
- ___ Become a Freelance Sales Agent (£9.99)
- ___ Become an Au Pair (£8.99)
- ___ Becoming a Father (£8.99)
- ___ Buy & Run a Shop (£8.99)
- ___ Buy & Run a Small Hotel (£8.99)
- ___ Buying a Personal Computer (£9.99)
- ___ Career Networking (£8.99)
- ___ Career Planning for Women (£8.99)
- ___ Cash from your Computer (£9.99)
- ___ Choosing a Nursing Home (£9.99)
- ___ Choosing a Package Holiday (£8.99)
- ___ Claim State Benefits (£9.99)
- ___ Collecting a Debt (£9.99)
- ___ Communicate at Work (£7.99)
- ___ Conduct Staff Appraisals (£7.99)
- ___ Conducting Effective Interviews (£8.99)
- ___ Coping with Self Assessment (£9.99)
- ___ Copyright & Law for Writers (£8.99)
- ___ Counsel People at Work (£7.99)
- ___ Creating a Twist in the Tale (£8.99)
- ___ Creative Writing (£9.99)
- ___ Critical Thinking for Students (£8.99)
- ___ Dealing with a Death in the Family (£9.99)
- ___ Do Voluntary Work Abroad (£8.99)
- ___ Do Your Own Advertising (£8.99)
- ___ Do Your Own PR (£8.99)
- ___ Doing Business Abroad (£10.99)
- ___ Doing Business on the Internet (£12.99)
- ___ Emigrate (£9.99)
- ___ Employ & Manage Staff (£8.99)
- ___ Find Temporary Work Abroad (£8.99)
- ___ Finding a Job in Canada (£9.99)
- ___ Finding a Job in Computers (£8.99)
- ___ Finding a Job in New Zealand (£9.99)
- ___ Finding a Job with a Future (£8.99)
- ___ Finding Work Overseas (£9.99)
- ___ Freelance DJ-ing (£8.99)
- ___ Freelance Teaching & Tutoring (£9.99)
- ___ Get a Job Abroad (£10.99)
- ___ Get a Job in America (£9.99)
- ___ Get a Job in Australia (£9.99)
- ___ Get a Job in Europe (£9.99)
- ___ Get a Job in France (£9.99)
- ___ Get a Job in Travel & Tourism (£8.99)
- ___ Get into Radio (£8.99)
- ___ Getting into Films & Television (£10.99)
- ___ Getting That Job (£8.99)
- ___ Getting your First Job (£8.99)
- ___ Going to University (£8.99)
- ___ Helping your Child to Read (£8.99)
- ___ How to Study & Learn (£8.99)
- ___ Investing in People (£9.99)
- ___ Investing in Stocks & Shares (£9.99)
- ___ Keep Business Accounts (£7.99)
- ___ Know Your Rights at Work (£8.99)
- ___ Live & Work in America (£9.99)
- ___ Live & Work in Australia (£12.99)
- ___ Live & Work in Germany (£9.99)
- ___ Live & Work in Greece (£9.99)
- ___ Live & Work in Italy (£8.99)
- ___ Live & Work in New Zealand (£9.99)
- ___ Live & Work in Portugal (£9.99)
- ___ Live & Work in the Gulf (£9.99)
- ___ Living & Working in Britain (£8.99)
- ___ Living & Working in China (£9.99)
- ___ Living & Working in Hong Kong (£10.99)
- ___ Living & Working in Israel (£10.99)
- ___ Living & Working in Saudi Arabia (£12.99)
- ___ Living & Working in the Netherlands (£9.99)
- ___ Making a Complaint (£8.99)
- ___ Making a Wedding Speech (£8.99)
- ___ Manage a Sales Team (£8.99)
- ___ Manage an Office (£8.99)
- ___ Manage Computers at Work (£8.99)
- ___ Manage People at Work (£8.99)
- ___ Manage Your Career (£8.99)
- ___ Managing Budgets & Cash Flows (£9.99)
- ___ Managing Meetings (£8.99)
- ___ Managing Your Personal Finances (£8.99)
- ___ Managing Yourself (£8.99)
- ___ Market Yourself (£8.99)
- ___ Master Book-Keeping (£8.99)
- ___ Mastering Business English (£8.99)
- ___ Master GCSE Accounts (£8.99)
- ___ Master Public Speaking (£8.99)
- ___ Migrating to Canada (£12.99)
- ___ Obtaining Visas & Work Permits (£9.99)
- ___ Organising Effective Training (£9.99)
- ___ Pass Exams Without Anxiety (£7.99)
- ___ Passing That Interview (£8.99)
- ___ Plan a Wedding (£7.99)
- ___ Planning Your Gap Year (£8.99)
- ___ Prepare a Business Plan (£8.99)
- ___ Publish a Book (£9.99)
- ___ Publish a Newsletter (£9.99)
- ___ Raise Funds & Sponsorship (£7.99)
- ___ Rent & Buy Property in France (£9.99)
- ___ Rent & Buy Property in Italy (£9.99)

How To Books

___ Research Methods (£8.99)
___ Retire Abroad (£8.99)
___ Return to Work (£7.99)
___ Run a Voluntary Group (£8.99)
___ Setting up Home in Florida (£9.99)
___ Spending a Year Abroad (£8.99)
___ Start a Business from Home (£7.99)
___ Start a New Career (£6.99)
___ Starting to Manage (£8.99)
___ Starting to Write (£8.99)
___ Start Word Processing (£8.99)
___ Start Your Own Business (£8.99)
___ Study Abroad (£8.99)
___ Study & Live in Britain (£7.99)
___ Studying at University (£8.99)
___ Studying for a Degree (£8.99)
___ Successful Grandparenting (£8.99)
___ Successful Mail Order Marketing (£9.99)
___ Successful Single Parenting (£8.99)
___ Survive Divorce (£8.99)
___ Surviving Redundancy (£8.99)
___ Taking in Students (£8.99)
___ Taking on Staff (£8.99)
___ Taking Your A-Levels (£8.99)
___ Teach Abroad (£8.99)
___ Teach Adults (£8.99)
___ Teaching Someone to Drive (£8.99)
___ Travel Round the World (£8.99)
___ Understand Finance at Work (£8.99)
___ Use a Library (£7.99)

___ Use the Internet (£9.99)
___ Winning Consumer Competitions (£8.99)
___ Winning Presentations (£8.99)
___ Work from Home (£8.99)
___ Work in an Office (£7.99)
___ Work in Retail (£8.99)
___ Work with Dogs (£8.99)
___ Working Abroad (£14.99)
___ Working as a Holiday Rep (£9.99)
___ Working in Japan (£10.99)
___ Working in Photography (£8.99)
___ Working in the Gulf (£10.99)
___ Working in Hotels & Catering (£9.99)
___ Working on Contract Worldwide (£9.99)
___ Working on Cruise Ships (£9.99)
___ Write a Press Release (£9.99)
___ Write a Report (£8.99)
___ Write an Assignment (£8.99)
___ Write & Sell Computer Software (£9.99)
___ Write for Publication (£8.99)
___ Write for Television (£8.99)
___ Writing a CV that Works (£8.99)
___ Writing a Non Fiction Book (£9.99)
___ Writing an Essay (£8.99)
___ Writing & Publishing Poetry (£9.99)
___ Writing & Selling a Novel (£8.99)
___ Writing Business Letters (£8.99)
___ Writing Reviews (£9.99)
___ Writing Your Dissertation (£8.99)

To: Plymbridge Distributors Ltd, Plymbridge House, Estover Road, Plymouth PL6 7PZ. Customer Services Tel: (01752) 202301. Fax: (01752) 202331.

Please send me copies of the titles I have indicated. Please add postage & packing (UK £1, Europe including Eire, £2, World £3 airmail).

☐ I enclose cheque/PO payable to Plymbridge Distributors Ltd for £ _____

☐ Please charge to my ☐ MasterCard, ☐ Visa, ☐ AMEX card.

Account No. ☐☐☐☐ ☐☐☐☐ ☐☐☐☐ ☐☐☐☐

Card Expiry Date ☐☐ ☐☐ 19   ☎ **Credit Card orders may be faxed or phoned.**

Customer Name (CAPITALS) ....

Address ....

.... Postcode ....

Telephone .... Signature ....

Every effort will be made to despatch your copy as soon as possible but to avoid possible disappointment please allow up to 21 days for despatch time (42 days if overseas). Prices and availability are subject to change without notice.

Code BPA